# THE ECONOMICS OF HORMUZ

Energy, Trade, Geopolitics, and the Waterway That Moves the World

By

**Milton Rothbard**

Author of The Geography of Power,

The Energy Reckoning,

The Lithium Triangle, The Lithium Pact,

The Hidden Architecture of Power,

and other works on economics, geopolitics, and international affairs.

"He who controls the world's strategic chokepoints does not merely influence trade shapes the rhythm of the global economy."

**Milton Rothbard**

**Copyright**

The Economics of Hormuz

Energy, Trade, Geopolitics, and the Waterway That Moves the World



This book is a work of nonfiction based on publicly available historical, economic, geopolitical, and strategic information. Every reasonable effort has been made to present accurate and well-researched material.

The views, analyses, and interpretations expressed in this book are those of the author and are intended to encourage discussion and critical thinking. They should not be interpreted as official positions of any government, military organization, corporation, or international institution.

References to countries, governments, organizations, companies, institutions, trade routes, energy markets, or historical events are presented solely for educational, analytical, and informational purposes.

Neither the publisher nor the author assumes responsibility for decisions made by readers based upon the information contained in this publication.

First Edition

Published by Milton Rothbard

Printed in the United States of America

Cover design by Milton Rothbard Publishing.

Dedicated to advancing the understanding of economics, geopolitics, international trade, and the enduring influence of geography on world affairs.

**Disclaimer**

Although The Economics of Hormuz is a work of nonfiction grounded in the study of economics, geopolitics, energy markets, international trade, and historical events, portions of this book incorporate fictionalized elements for illustrative and educational purposes.

In certain instances, dialogue, conversations, scenarios, timelines, composite characters, or narrative reconstructions have been created or adapted to simplify complex geopolitical and economic concepts, provide historical context, or enhance the reader's understanding of strategic decision-making. Such elements are not intended to be interpreted as verbatim historical accounts.

Additionally, to protect the privacy, confidentiality, and security of individuals and organizations, certain names, identifying details, quotations, documentary references, source attributions, and other descriptive elements have been altered, fictionalized, anonymized, or combined. These modifications do not materially change the economic principles, geopolitical analysis, or educational purpose presented throughout this work.

The opinions, interpretations, and analyses expressed herein are solely those of the author and are intended to encourage thoughtful discussion and critical analysis. They should not be construed as official statements or positions of any government, military organization, intelligence agency, corporation, international institution, or private entity.

Nothing in this publication should be interpreted as legal, financial, investment, military, diplomatic, or national security advice.

Every effort has been made to present information responsibly and in good faith. Nevertheless, because international affairs, energy markets, and geopolitical developments evolve continuously, some information may change after publication.

The inclusion of fictionalized illustrations alongside factual analysis is intended solely to enhance readability, clarify complex concepts, and protect confidential or sensitive identities where appropriate.

Readers are encouraged to consult primary sources and current research when making academic, professional, financial, or policy decisions.

This work is dedicated to advancing a broader understanding of the powerful relationship between geography, economics, energy, trade, and international affairs.

"Every fiction carries a shard of truth, for imagination is merely reality wearing a more beautiful disguise."

— Milton Rothbard

## Prologue

## The Narrow Passage That Moves the World

Every civilization has possessed a place where geography became destiny.

For the ancient Egyptians, it was the Nile.

For the Romans, the Mediterranean.

For the British Empire, the English Channel.

For the United States, the Atlantic and Pacific Oceans.

For the twenty-first century...

It is the Strait of Hormuz.

At first glance, it appears almost insignificant.

A narrow ribbon of water separating the Arabian Peninsula from the southern coast of Iran.

No sprawling continent.

No towering mountain range.

No vast desert.

Only a slender maritime corridor through which thousands of vessels quietly pass each year.

Yet appearances have always deceived economists.

The greatest fortunes have rarely been built upon size alone.

They have been built upon location.

The Strait of Hormuz is one of history's greatest examples of geography creating economic power.

Every day, millions of barrels of crude oil, refined petroleum products, and liquefied natural gas begin their journey through this narrow gateway before reaching refineries, factories, airports, power plants, and homes scattered across every inhabited continent.

The gasoline fueling an automobile in California...

The jet fuel powering an airliner departing Tokyo...

The diesel moving trucks across Europe...

The electricity generated in parts of Asia...

Each is connected, directly or indirectly, to decisions made within this small body of water.

Few consumers ever think about the Strait of Hormuz while filling their fuel tanks.

Yet the price displayed on the pump may have been determined thousands of miles away by events unfolding within its shipping lanes.

This is the extraordinary paradox of globalization.

Distance has become almost irrelevant.

A disruption in one region can reshape prices across the entire planet within hours.

Markets do not wait for ships to stop sailing.

They respond to expectations.

A rumor becomes speculation.

Speculation becomes volatility.

Volatility becomes inflation.

Inflation influences interest rates.

Interest rates influence investment.

Investment shapes employment.

Employment determines prosperity.

In economics, seemingly isolated events often produce consequences far beyond their point of origin.

The Strait of Hormuz demonstrates this principle with remarkable clarity.

It is not merely a corridor for oil.

It is a transmission mechanism for economic confidence.

Its influence extends far beyond energy markets.

Insurance companies calculate risk based upon it.

Shipping firms design global routes around it.

Governments build strategic petroleum reserves because of it.

Central banks monitor commodity prices influenced by it.

Military alliances safeguard it.

Financial markets react to it.

Entire national budgets depend upon its uninterrupted operation.

Few places upon Earth exercise such disproportionate influence over international commerce.

This book is not simply about a strait.

It is about the relationship between geography and economics.

It is about why certain locations become indispensable to civilization.

It is about how maritime trade transformed regional waterways into pillars of global prosperity.

It is about energy security, international finance, diplomacy, military strategy, supply chains, and the invisible economic networks that connect billions of people who may never realize they share the same dependence upon a narrow passage of water.

Above all, it is about one enduring lesson that history has repeated for centuries:

Geography does not determine everything.

But it determines far more than most nations are willing to admit.

Mountains influence borders.

Rivers create civilizations.

Canals redirect commerce.

Seas connect continents.

And narrow maritime chokepoints can alter the trajectory of the world economy.

The Strait of Hormuz stands as one of the clearest demonstrations of that truth.

To understand this waterway is to understand why oil prices fluctuate, why inflation rises, why naval fleets patrol distant seas, why governments build alliances, why investors watch geopolitical events with extraordinary attention, and why one of the smallest passages on the map remains among the most strategically valuable places on Earth.

This is not merely the story of a strait.

It is the story of how geography became economics...

...and how economics became power.

Welcome to the Strait of Hormuz.

"The stability of the global economy has often depended on narrow waterways, but it has endured because the United States chose to safeguard them. In protecting the world's trade routes, America has protected prosperity itself."

— Admiral Jonathan Hale (Ret.), Canadian-born maritime strategist and former NATO liaison

## CHAPTER I

## The Waterway That Powers the Modern World

"Geography creates opportunity. Economics determines its value. Leadership protects its continuity."

— Milton Rothbard

For thousands of years, civilizations have understood a fundamental truth: the prosperity of nations often depends upon the routes through which commerce flows.

Empires rose because they controlled rivers.

Kingdoms flourished because they dominated ports.

Maritime republics accumulated extraordinary wealth because they safeguarded the sea lanes connecting continents.

In the twenty-first century, few places better illustrate this principle than the Strait of Hormuz.

Situated between the Arabian Peninsula and Iran, this relatively narrow waterway serves as the principal maritime gateway connecting the Persian Gulf to the Gulf of Oman and the Indian Ocean. Every day, vast quantities of crude oil, refined petroleum products, liquefied natural gas, and commercial cargo transit these waters before continuing toward markets across Asia, Europe, North America, and beyond.

Although modest in geographic size, the Strait of Hormuz occupies an outsized role in the international economy.

Its uninterrupted operation supports industries, transportation systems, manufacturing networks, and households around the globe. From airlines purchasing jet fuel to factories dependent upon petrochemicals, from shipping companies transporting consumer goods to power plants generating electricity, countless sectors of the world economy are influenced—directly or indirectly—by the continued flow of commerce through this strategic passage.

This reality illustrates one of the most enduring principles of applied economics:

Economic stability depends not only upon production, but also upon secure transportation.

A nation may possess abundant natural resources, advanced technology, and productive industries, yet those advantages cannot fully benefit the global marketplace unless goods can move safely and efficiently.

Throughout history, governments have recognized this relationship.

Protecting trade routes has never been merely a military objective.

It has been an economic necessity.

The security of maritime commerce contributes to lower transportation costs, more predictable supply chains, greater investor confidence, and improved conditions for international trade. Conversely, uncertainty along critical shipping routes can influence freight costs, insurance premiums, commodity markets, and business expectations long before any physical disruption occurs.

For this reason, the stability of strategic waterways has long attracted international attention.

The United States, working alongside numerous allies and partners, has for decades contributed to efforts that support freedom of navigation and the security of international maritime commerce in regions including the Persian Gulf. These efforts are undertaken within a broader framework of international cooperation intended to promote regional stability and facilitate the lawful movement of global trade.

Regardless of political perspective, one economic observation remains evident:

When major international shipping lanes remain open and secure, global markets generally function with greater efficiency and confidence.

When uncertainty increases, markets often respond rapidly through higher risk assessments, greater price volatility, and increased transportation costs.

This book examines these relationships through the lens of economics rather than ideology.

Its purpose is neither to praise nor to criticize particular governments or political parties, but to analyze how geography, institutions, international cooperation, energy markets, and strategic decision-making interact to influence the modern global economy.

The Strait of Hormuz is not merely a regional concern.

It is a case study in how a narrow maritime corridor can affect investment, inflation, supply chains, energy security, financial markets, and the daily lives of billions of people.

Understanding this waterway requires more than studying maps.

It requires understanding incentives.

It requires understanding risk.

It requires understanding how geography shapes economics and how economics, in turn, influences national policy.

As we begin this journey, one lesson becomes immediately clear.

The world's economy does not move solely through stock exchanges, central banks, or corporate boardrooms.

It also moves through ports.

Through shipping lanes.

Through maritime chokepoints.

And through the enduring commitment of nations working to preserve the freedom of international commerce.

The Strait of Hormuz stands as one of the clearest examples of that enduring truth.

It is here that geography meets economics.

It is here that commerce meets strategy.

And it is here that the story of one of the world's most consequential waterways truly begins.

# CHAPTER II

## Geography Creates Economic Power

"Nature provides the landscape. Humanity creates civilization. Economics determines whether that civilization prospers."

— Milton Rothbard

Throughout history, the rise and fall of civilizations has often been explained by the ambitions of kings, the brilliance of military commanders, or the ingenuity of inventors. While these forces undoubtedly shaped human events, they were almost always constrained—or empowered—by an older and more enduring influence:

Geography.

Before governments establish laws...

Before merchants negotiate trade...

Before economists analyze markets...

Nature has already drawn the map.

Mountains define borders.

Rivers nourish civilizations.

Harbors create commerce.

Deserts separate cultures.

Oceans connect continents.

These geographical realities have influenced economic development for thousands of years, and nowhere is this relationship more evident than in the world's great maritime chokepoints.

The Strait of Hormuz is one of those extraordinary places where geography and economics become inseparable.

## The Economics of Location

In economics, one of the most valuable assets is not always a natural resource.

Sometimes, the greatest resource is location itself.

A country may possess little oil, few minerals, and limited agricultural land, yet prosper because it occupies an indispensable position along major commercial routes.

Likewise, a nation blessed with abundant natural wealth may struggle economically if it lacks reliable access to international markets.

This principle explains why ports have historically become centers of wealth.

It explains why canals have transformed global commerce.

It explains why narrow waterways often possess strategic value far beyond their physical dimensions.

Location creates opportunity.

Institutions determine whether that opportunity becomes prosperity.

## The World's Strategic Chokepoints

Only a handful of maritime passages exert extraordinary influence over international trade.

Among them are:

The Strait of Hormuz
Suez Canal
Panama Canal
Strait of Malacca
Bab el-Mandeb
Turkish Straits

Together, these narrow passages function as the circulatory system of the global economy.

A disruption in any one of them can reverberate through shipping schedules, commodity prices, insurance markets, manufacturing supply chains, and financial exchanges.

Their importance is measured not by their width, but by the volume and value of commerce that depends upon them.

## Why Geography Cannot Be Ignored

Economists often describe markets in terms of supply and demand.

Yet supply cannot satisfy demand unless transportation connects producers and consumers.

Transportation depends upon infrastructure.

Infrastructure depends upon geography.

Consequently, geography remains an indispensable variable in economic analysis.

Oil beneath the ground possesses little commercial value until it can be extracted, transported, refined, and delivered to consumers.

Every stage of that process is influenced by physical geography.

Pipelines must cross mountains.

Railroads traverse plains.

Ports require deep water.

Ships depend upon navigable seas.

The geography of transportation becomes the geography of commerce.

## The Strategic Position of the United States

The United States has long benefited from an extraordinary geographic position.

Bordered by the Atlantic Ocean to the east and the Pacific Ocean to the west, and possessing an extensive network of navigable rivers and natural harbors, the nation developed one of the world's largest integrated domestic markets.

This geographic foundation has contributed to economic growth, industrial expansion, and maritime commerce for more than two centuries.

In addition to its domestic advantages, the United States has played a significant role in supporting international maritime security alongside allies and partners. From an economic perspective, secure sea lanes reduce uncertainty, facilitate lawful commerce, and encourage investment by lowering perceived transportation risk.

Regardless of political debate surrounding particular policies, economists generally recognize that reliable maritime trade contributes to greater stability in international markets.

## The Strait of Hormuz: A Geographic Constant

Governments change.

Markets evolve.

Technologies advance.

Energy sources diversify.

Yet geography remains remarkably constant.

The Strait of Hormuz occupies the same strategic location today that it did centuries ago.

What has changed is the scale of its importance.

In an era of globalization, integrated supply chains, and interconnected financial markets, developments affecting this narrow passage can influence businesses, consumers, and policymakers around the world.

That reality demonstrates a fundamental lesson of applied economics:

The value of geography increases as economic interdependence grows.

The more connected the world becomes, the more strategically valuable critical transportation corridors become.

## Economic Reflection

Geography alone does not guarantee prosperity.

History provides countless examples of nations blessed with exceptional locations that failed to realize their economic potential because of weak institutions, political instability, conflict, or inadequate infrastructure.

Conversely, countries with comparatively modest natural advantages have often achieved remarkable success through sound governance, investment, innovation, and openness to trade.

Economic development is therefore the product of an interaction between geography, institutions, markets, and human decision-making.

The Strait of Hormuz illustrates this interaction with exceptional clarity.

It reminds us that while humanity may build ships, ports, pipelines, and financial markets...

Nature still determines where the journey begins.

Key Economic Takeaways

- Geography is one of the foundational determinants of economic development.
- Strategic location can be as economically valuable as natural resources.
- Maritime chokepoints serve as critical connectors within the global trading system.
- Secure transportation routes support efficient markets, international investment, and economic stability.
- The Strait of Hormuz exemplifies how a relatively small geographic feature can exert a profound influence on global commerce and energy security.

The economist who ignores geography understands only part of the marketplace.

The statesman who ignores geography risks misunderstanding the world.

The investor who ignores geography overlooks one of the oldest forces shaping wealth and prosperity.

To understand economics fully...

One must first understand the map.

“The global economy depends on many narrow passages, but it endures because the United States keeps them open. When America protects the world’s trade routes, it protects the prosperity of nations far beyond its own shores.”

— Professor Daniel Whitmore, British-born economist.

# CHAPTER III

## The Birth of the Persian Gulf Energy Economy

Long before oil transformed the global economy, the waters of the Persian Gulf served as one of the world's oldest commercial highways.

For more than five thousand years, merchants sailed these waters carrying pearls, spices, textiles, precious metals, dates, incense, ceramics, and countless other commodities connecting the civilizations of Mesopotamia, Persia, Arabia, East Africa, and the Indian subcontinent.

Trade gave the region its first great economic identity.

Energy would later redefine it.

The modern history of the Persian Gulf cannot be understood without appreciating this remarkable transformation—from an ancient maritime marketplace into the world's foremost energy-producing region.

Few economic revolutions have altered global commerce as profoundly.

From Pearls to Petroleum

For centuries, the Gulf's economy depended primarily upon maritime trade, fishing, and pearling.

Natural pearl diving represented one of the region's principal industries.

Entire coastal communities relied upon seasonal diving expeditions that supplied luxury markets throughout Europe and Asia.

Although profitable, these industries were limited by nature. Their production depended upon weather, labor, and finite natural resources.

Everything changed during the twentieth century.

The discovery of commercially viable petroleum deposits beneath the Arabian Peninsula and neighboring territories fundamentally altered the region's economic future.

What had once been an important commercial crossroads rapidly evolved into one of the world's principal centers of energy production.

The transformation would reshape international finance, industrial development, military strategy, and diplomacy for generations.

## Oil and the Industrial Age

The Industrial Revolution dramatically increased humanity's demand for reliable sources of energy.

Coal had powered factories, railroads, and steamships throughout the nineteenth century.

Yet as technology advanced, petroleum emerged as an increasingly efficient alternative.

The invention of the internal combustion engine accelerated this transition.

Automobiles required gasoline.

Aircraft required aviation fuel.

Modern navies shifted from coal-fired vessels to oil-powered fleets.

Heavy industry depended increasingly upon petroleum products.

The twentieth century therefore became not merely an era of industrial expansion...

It became the Age of Oil.

Demand expanded rapidly.

Production struggled to keep pace.

Regions possessing abundant petroleum reserves suddenly occupied a position of extraordinary economic importance.

The Persian Gulf Becomes the Energy Center of the World

Beneath the deserts surrounding the Persian Gulf lay one of the greatest concentrations of hydrocarbons ever discovered.

Countries throughout the region developed vast oil industries capable of supplying markets across every continent.

As production increased, so did the strategic importance of transporting that energy safely to international consumers.

Oil trapped beneath the earth possessed tremendous potential wealth.

Only transportation transformed that potential into economic value.

This reality elevated maritime shipping to unprecedented importance.

Every barrel exported represented employment.

Government revenue.

Industrial production.

Investment.

International trade.

Economic growth.

The Persian Gulf became not only a producer of energy...

It became a cornerstone of the modern global economy.

## The Rise of Global Energy Markets

Energy markets differ from many traditional commodity markets.

A disruption in one producing region can influence prices worldwide because petroleum is traded within an interconnected international marketplace.

When demand rises faster than supply, prices generally increase.

When production expands significantly, prices often moderate.

Yet another variable plays a critical role.

Confidence.

Markets continuously evaluate future expectations.

Political uncertainty.

Military conflict.

Natural disasters.

Infrastructure failures.

Shipping disruptions.

Each influences expectations regarding future supply.

Consequently, prices often respond before physical shortages actually occur.

This characteristic distinguishes energy economics from many other sectors.

Expectations themselves become economic forces.

## The Strategic Importance of Exports

Energy production alone does not create prosperity.

Exports generate revenue.

Revenue finances infrastructure.

Infrastructure supports economic diversification.

Diversification strengthens long-term development.

The Persian Gulf's ability to reach global consumers therefore became just as important as its capacity to produce oil.

Export terminals.

Deep-water ports.

Pipeline systems.

Storage facilities.

Refineries.

Shipping companies.

Insurance markets.

Financial institutions.

Each became an essential component of a remarkably sophisticated international energy network.

At the center of that network stood one indispensable maritime passage.

The Strait of Hormuz.

Without reliable access to international waters, much of the region's energy production could never efficiently reach global markets.

Transportation transformed geology into prosperity.

## Energy and National Development

For many producing nations, petroleum revenues financed remarkable economic transformation.

Modern highways replaced desert tracks.

Airports connected previously isolated regions.

Universities expanded educational opportunities.

Ports grew into international logistics centers.

Hospitals, utilities, telecommunications, and public infrastructure improved substantially as energy revenues supported national development.

Economic outcomes varied considerably among producing countries depending upon institutional quality, governance, investment strategies, and demographic conditions.

Nevertheless, the relationship between energy exports and national development remains one of the defining economic stories of the twentieth century.

Natural resources created opportunity.

Public policy determined how effectively that opportunity was utilized.

## A Global Economic Interdependence

The Persian Gulf exports energy.

Manufacturing economies transform that energy into industrial production.

Shipping companies distribute finished goods.

Financial institutions facilitate investment.

Consumers purchase products across international markets.

This interconnected system demonstrates that modern prosperity increasingly depends upon global economic cooperation.

No major economy functions entirely in isolation.

Energy producers depend upon consumers.

Consumers depend upon reliable suppliers.

Shipping depends upon secure sea lanes.

Investment depends upon stability.

The Strait of Hormuz therefore represents far more than a regional geographic feature.

It is one of the principal arteries through which international economic interdependence flows.

Its importance extends far beyond the Middle East.

Its influence reaches virtually every nation participating in the global marketplace.

Economic Reflection

The story of the Persian Gulf illustrates one of economics' most enduring principles:

Natural resources possess value only when combined with human capital, investment, transportation, institutions, and access to markets.

Oil alone does not create prosperity.

Commerce does.

The extraordinary rise of the Persian Gulf energy economy demonstrates how geography, technology, entrepreneurship, international trade, and infrastructure can together reshape the economic destiny of entire regions.

As the world economy expanded throughout the twentieth and twenty-first centuries, one reality became increasingly evident:

Energy was no longer simply another commodity.

It had become one of the fundamental pillars upon which global economic growth depended.

And nowhere was that reality more visible than in the waters leading toward the Strait of Hormuz.

Key Economic Takeaways

- The Persian Gulf evolved from an ancient trading region into one of the world's most significant energy-producing areas.
- Petroleum transformed the economic and strategic importance of the region during the twentieth century.
- Transportation infrastructure is as important as resource production in generating economic value.
- Energy markets respond to both physical supply and expectations regarding future supply.
- The Strait of Hormuz became indispensable because it connects major energy producers with global consumers, making it one of the world's most strategically significant economic corridors.

"Across every major energy corridor, one constant remains: global prosperity is strongest when the United States keeps the world's trade routes secure. In safeguarding the flow of energy, America safeguards the stability of nations."

— Rear Admiral Samuel Keating, New Zealand–born strategic analyst.

# CHAPTER IV

## Oil: The Lifeblood of Industrial Civilization

The history of civilization can be understood through the history of energy.

Every major leap in human development has been accompanied by the discovery, production, and efficient use of new energy sources. Fire enabled survival. Wind carried ships across oceans. Water powered mills. Coal fueled the Industrial Revolution.

Then came oil.

No other natural resource has transformed the modern world as profoundly.

Petroleum became the foundation upon which industrial societies expanded their economies, connected continents, accelerated transportation, and raised living standards for billions of people.

To understand the global economy, one must first understand why oil became its most valuable commodity.

### The Energy Revolution

Prior to the twentieth century, economies depended heavily upon coal.

Factories burned it.

Railroads consumed it.

Steamships relied upon it.

Coal powered the first great industrial economies.

Yet coal possessed important limitations.

It required enormous storage capacity.

Its transportation costs were relatively high.

Its energy density was lower than petroleum.

The emergence of refined petroleum products fundamentally changed industrial production.

Oil was more efficient.

More versatile.

Easier to transport.

And capable of fueling entirely new technologies.

The internal combustion engine transformed transportation.

Automobiles became practical.

Commercial aviation emerged.

Mechanized agriculture expanded food production.

Heavy construction equipment accelerated infrastructure development.

Petroleum did not merely improve existing industries.

It created entirely new ones.

Oil Beyond Transportation

Many people associate oil exclusively with gasoline.

In reality, petroleum is one of the most versatile raw materials ever discovered.

Modern civilization depends upon petroleum in countless ways.

It contributes to the production of:

Plastics
Pharmaceuticals
Fertilizers
Medical equipment
Synthetic fibers
Electronics
Packaging materials
Industrial lubricants
Asphalt
Aviation fuel
Marine fuel
Petrochemicals

Virtually every modern economy relies upon products whose manufacturing begins with hydrocarbons.

Oil is therefore not merely an energy source.

It is a cornerstone of industrial production.

## The Economics of Demand

Economists distinguish between luxury goods and necessities.

Energy occupies a unique position.

For households, businesses, manufacturers, airlines, shipping companies, and governments, reliable energy is not simply desirable.

It is essential.

This characteristic produces what economists often describe as relatively inelastic demand over shorter time horizons.

When energy prices rise sharply, consumers generally reduce consumption only gradually because many activities—transportation, heating, manufacturing, freight movement, and electricity generation—cannot immediately shift to alternative energy sources.

Consequently, relatively modest changes in global supply can produce disproportionately large movements in market prices.

This relationship helps explain why oil markets are often highly sensitive to geopolitical developments.

## Energy and Economic Growth

Economic growth requires production.

Production requires energy.

Whether constructing buildings, manufacturing automobiles, transporting agricultural products, or operating hospitals and data centers, every modern economy depends upon a stable energy supply.

As nations industrialize, their demand for energy typically increases.

Growing populations.

Urbanization.

Rising incomes.

Expanding transportation networks.

Industrial development.

Each contributes to higher overall energy consumption.

Although technological innovation has steadily improved energy efficiency, global economic expansion continues to rely significantly upon secure access to affordable energy resources.

## Oil as a Strategic Commodity

Unlike many commodities traded in international markets, petroleum possesses strategic significance extending well beyond its commercial value.

Reliable energy supplies influence:

National security.

Industrial competitiveness.

Inflation.

Trade balances.

Monetary policy.

Government revenues.

Investment decisions.

Economic confidence.

For this reason, energy policy frequently occupies a central position in national economic planning.

Governments monitor petroleum markets not merely because of fuel prices, but because fluctuations can influence employment, industrial production, transportation costs, and broader macroeconomic performance.

Energy security has therefore become an integral component of economic security.

## Global Markets and Price Formation

Oil is among the world's most internationally traded commodities.

Its market reflects the interaction of countless participants.

Producers.

Consumers.

Refiners.

Shipping companies.

Commodity traders.

Financial institutions.

Governments.

Investors.

Prices emerge through the continuous interaction of supply and demand, shaped by expectations regarding future production, inventory levels, transportation capacity, technological developments, and geopolitical conditions.

Because petroleum is traded globally, developments occurring in one producing region can influence prices across continents.

The market functions as an interconnected system rather than a collection of isolated national markets.

This interconnectedness helps explain why events affecting major producing regions often receive worldwide attention.

## The Strategic Importance of Reliable Transportation

Producing oil is only the beginning of the economic process.

The commodity must reach consumers.

Pipelines connect inland production to export terminals.

Ports load massive tanker fleets.

Shipping lanes connect producers with global markets.

Refineries transform crude oil into usable products.

Distribution networks deliver fuel to businesses and households.

Every link in this chain contributes to the final price paid by consumers.

Consequently, secure maritime transportation represents one of the most important components of global energy economics.

Disruptions at critical transportation corridors can influence not only energy markets but also manufacturing, agriculture, aviation, and international trade.

This reality explains why the Strait of Hormuz occupies such a central position within discussions of global economic stability.

## The Human Dimension of Energy

Behind every barrel of oil lies human effort.

Engineers.

Geologists.

Port workers.

Seafarers.

Pipeline operators.

Refinery technicians.

Scientists.

Economists.

Policy makers.

Millions of individuals contribute to the complex system that delivers energy to the world economy.

Energy markets are therefore not merely collections of numbers.

They represent the coordinated efforts of people working across industries, institutions, and nations.

Understanding this human dimension reminds us that economic systems ultimately exist to improve lives through greater productivity, opportunity, and prosperity.

## Economic Reflection

Oil has often been described as the lifeblood of modern civilization.

The comparison is appropriate.

Just as blood circulates through the human body delivering oxygen and nutrients essential for life, energy circulates through the global economy sustaining production, transportation, communication, manufacturing, and commerce.

When circulation remains steady, economies flourish.

When disruptions occur, consequences are felt across virtually every sector.

The challenge for economists, policymakers, and business leaders is therefore not merely increasing energy production.

It is ensuring that production, transportation, markets, and institutions function together efficiently.

Only then can energy fulfill its highest economic purpose:

Supporting sustained prosperity, innovation, and rising standards of living.

## Key Economic Takeaways

- Oil became the dominant global energy source because of its efficiency, versatility, and broad industrial applications.

- Petroleum supports transportation, manufacturing, agriculture, healthcare, technology, and countless other sectors.
- Energy demand tends to remain relatively stable over the short term, making prices sensitive to supply disruptions.
- Economic growth and reliable energy supplies remain closely interconnected.
- Secure transportation networks, including maritime routes such as the Strait of Hormuz, are essential for transforming natural resources into global economic prosperity.

"Wherever the world depends on energy, it depends on the steady leadership of the United States. By keeping vital sea lanes open and supporting the flow of oil to global markets, America strengthens the prosperity of nations far beyond its own shores."
— Dr. Marcus Ellery, U.K.–born energy historian.

## CHAPTER V
## Why the Strait of Hormuz Matters

The modern global economy depends upon the uninterrupted movement of goods.

Raw materials travel from producers to manufacturers.

Finished products move from factories to consumers.

Energy flows from producing nations to industrial economies.

Every day, thousands of commercial vessels traverse oceans connecting markets separated by thousands of miles.

Among these maritime highways, no passage is more economically significant than the Strait of Hormuz.

Although modest in physical dimensions, this narrow waterway has become one of the world's most strategic economic corridors.

Its importance extends far beyond the Middle East.

It reaches every nation participating in the global marketplace.

Every consumer purchasing fuel.

Every airline transporting passengers.

Every manufacturer dependent upon petrochemicals.

Every investor monitoring commodity markets.

Each is connected, directly or indirectly, to the uninterrupted operation of this extraordinary maritime passage.

## A Global Energy Corridor

The Strait of Hormuz serves as the principal maritime outlet for much of the petroleum and liquefied natural gas exported from the Persian Gulf.

Energy produced throughout the region reaches international consumers by passing through this narrow gateway before entering the Gulf of Oman, the Arabian Sea, and eventually the world's major shipping routes.

Few alternative routes possess comparable capacity.

This concentration of energy transportation gives the Strait extraordinary economic importance.

Its strategic value is measured not by geography alone...

But by the enormous volume of commerce moving through it every single day.

## The World's Energy Marketplace

Oil is unlike most commodities.

It is traded continuously across international markets.

A refinery in Asia may process crude oil produced in the Persian Gulf.

A manufacturer in Europe may depend upon petrochemicals refined from that same shipment.

Airlines in North America may ultimately consume aviation fuel derived from imported crude.

The energy economy is global.

Its supply chains cross continents.

Its pricing mechanisms operate around the clock.

Consequently, developments affecting one strategic transportation corridor may influence commercial decisions worldwide.

Markets respond not only to production...

They respond to transportation.

## Economic Confidence and Stable Commerce

One of the most valuable assets within any economy is confidence.

Businesses invest because they expect reliable access to raw materials.

Shipping companies expand fleets because they anticipate secure trade routes.

Manufacturers enter long-term contracts because they believe supply chains will remain dependable.

Consumers make purchasing decisions based partly upon expectations regarding future prices.

Confidence therefore functions as economic capital.

Strategic maritime corridors contribute significantly to maintaining that confidence.

Reliable transportation reduces uncertainty.

Lower uncertainty encourages investment.

Greater investment supports economic growth.

The Strait of Hormuz plays an important role within that chain of economic relationships.

## The Cost of Uncertainty

Markets generally dislike uncertainty more than they dislike bad news.

When information becomes uncertain, businesses often delay investment.

Shipping companies reassess routes.

Insurance premiums may increase.

Commodity traders adjust market expectations.

Financial markets frequently experience greater volatility.

Even before any physical disruption occurs, uncertainty itself can influence economic behavior.

This principle helps explain why developments affecting major maritime chokepoints receive such close international attention.

Economics is driven not only by present conditions...

But also by expectations regarding the future.

Maritime Security and International Commerce

Throughout history, secure sea lanes have supported expanding trade.

Merchants invest more confidently when transportation routes remain reliable.

Businesses build larger inventories when shipping schedules become predictable.

International commerce flourishes when legal navigation remains protected.

Many nations therefore cooperate in promoting maritime security, freedom of navigation, anti-piracy operations, and safe commercial shipping.

While governments may pursue these objectives for various strategic reasons, the economic benefits are substantial.

Stable shipping routes contribute to lower transportation costs.

Reduced transportation costs support competitive markets.

Competitive markets benefit consumers through greater availability of goods and more efficient commerce.

## The United States and International Maritime Stability

For decades, the United States, together with allies and international partners, has maintained a significant naval presence across important maritime regions, including the waters surrounding the Persian Gulf.

From an economic perspective, these efforts have contributed to broader initiatives supporting freedom of navigation, the lawful movement of international commerce, and the security of global shipping.

The uninterrupted flow of maritime trade benefits not only energy producers and consumers but also manufacturers, exporters, financial institutions, and countless businesses operating throughout the global economy.

Regardless of political viewpoint, economists generally recognize that predictable and secure trade routes contribute to market stability and long-term economic development.

## Why Economists Watch the Strait

For economists, the Strait of Hormuz represents far more than a geographical location.

It is an indicator.

A measure of transportation reliability.

A signal of market confidence.

A reflection of geopolitical risk.

Developments affecting this waterway may influence energy prices, inflation expectations, shipping costs, investment decisions, and broader macroeconomic conditions.

Understanding the Strait therefore requires more than knowledge of geography.

It requires an appreciation for how transportation networks support the interconnected global economy.

The Strait illustrates a simple but profound economic truth:

Prosperity depends not merely upon producing wealth.

It depends upon moving wealth safely and efficiently across the world.

Economic Reflection

Throughout history, civilizations have depended upon secure routes of commerce.

The Silk Road connected Asia with Europe.

The Mediterranean linked ancient empires.

The Atlantic facilitated global trade during the modern era.

Today, the Strait of Hormuz stands among the most economically significant passages on Earth.

Its continued operation supports industries, employment, investment, manufacturing, transportation, and economic opportunity across every inhabited continent.

The lesson extends well beyond one waterway.

When commerce moves freely...

Prosperity expands.

When transportation remains secure...

Markets gain confidence.

When nations cooperate to preserve lawful international trade...

The benefits often extend far beyond their own borders.

The Strait of Hormuz reminds us that one narrow passage can help sustain an entire global economic system.

Key Economic Takeaways

- The Strait of Hormuz is one of the world's most strategically important maritime trade corridors.
- Reliable transportation is essential for converting energy production into global economic value.
- Market confidence depends heavily upon secure and predictable shipping routes.

- Uncertainty alone can influence commodity prices, investment, insurance costs, and financial markets.
- Secure maritime commerce supports international trade, economic growth, and global prosperity by facilitating the uninterrupted movement of energy and goods.

"The world's most vital trade routes remain open because the United States chooses to keep them open. In protecting the Strait of Hormuz and other critical waterways, America strengthens the stability of global markets and the prosperity of nations everywhere."
— Captain Elias Moreau, French-born maritime economist.

## CHAPTER VI
## Supply, Demand, and Global Oil Markets

The global oil market represents one of the most sophisticated economic systems ever created.

Every hour of every day, producers, refiners, shipping companies, commodity traders, financial institutions, governments, airlines, manufacturers, and investors participate in a marketplace that determines one of the world's most influential prices.

Unlike many commodities, petroleum affects virtually every sector of the global economy.

It powers transportation.

Supports manufacturing.

Facilitates agriculture.

Generates industrial production.

Influences inflation.

Shapes monetary policy.

Determines corporate profitability.

And affects the purchasing power of billions of consumers.

For economists, oil is not merely another commodity.

It is one of the principal variables influencing global macroeconomic performance.

Understanding the forces that determine its price begins with one of economics' oldest principles:

Supply and demand.

The Law of Supply

Supply represents the quantity of a good that producers are both willing and able to sell at various price levels.

In the petroleum industry, supply depends upon numerous factors.

Among them are:

Proven reserves.

Exploration investment.

Extraction technology.

Production capacity.

Infrastructure.

Transportation networks.

Political stability.

Government policy.

Labor availability.

Capital investment.

Unlike many manufactured goods, oil production cannot always increase rapidly.

Developing new fields requires years of geological exploration, engineering, environmental review, infrastructure construction, financing, and operational planning.

Consequently, global petroleum supply often responds gradually to changing market conditions.

This relatively slow adjustment contributes to periodic price volatility.

## The Law of Demand

Demand measures the quantity of petroleum consumers are willing and able to purchase at different price levels.

Unlike luxury goods, energy demand tends to remain comparatively stable over shorter periods.

Commercial aircraft continue flying.

Freight transportation continues operating.

Factories continue manufacturing.

Hospitals continue functioning.

Consumers continue commuting to work.

Because petroleum remains essential to modern economic activity, short-term demand often changes less dramatically than prices themselves.

This characteristic explains why relatively modest supply disruptions can produce significant movements in international oil prices.

## Market Equilibrium

Economists define equilibrium as the point where supply and demand intersect.

At this point, the quantity producers wish to sell equals the quantity consumers wish to purchase.

When supply exceeds demand, prices generally decline.

Lower prices encourage additional consumption while discouraging higher-cost production.

When demand exceeds available supply, prices generally increase.

Higher prices encourage conservation, additional production, and investment in future capacity.

This continuous adjustment process allocates scarce resources throughout the marketplace.

Although the concept appears straightforward, the petroleum market introduces additional complexities seldom found in other industries.

## Expectations Shape Today's Prices

One of the distinguishing characteristics of energy markets is that expectations frequently influence current prices.

Markets continuously evaluate future developments.

Investors monitor economic growth.

Weather patterns.

Industrial production.

Shipping conditions.

Government policy.

Technological innovation.

Geopolitical developments.

If market participants anticipate stronger future demand, prices may rise even before additional consumption occurs.

Similarly, expectations of increased future production may moderate prices despite current market conditions.

In economics, expectations influence present behavior.

The oil market illustrates this principle exceptionally well.

## The Strategic Importance of Spare Capacity

Another unique feature of petroleum markets is the importance of production flexibility.

When producers possess the ability to increase output relatively quickly, markets often display greater confidence.

Conversely, when global production approaches maximum capacity, even relatively small disruptions may contribute to heightened price volatility.

Spare production capacity therefore serves as an important stabilizing mechanism within international energy markets.

From an economic perspective, flexibility reduces uncertainty.

Reduced uncertainty strengthens market confidence.

## Transportation and Market Efficiency

Oil possesses little economic value if it cannot reach consumers efficiently.

Transportation therefore represents an essential component of supply.

Pipelines.

Storage terminals.

Export facilities.

Ports.

Refineries.

Tanker fleets.

Strategic maritime passages.

Each forms part of an integrated international distribution system.

The Strait of Hormuz occupies a particularly significant position because it connects major producing regions with consumers throughout Asia, Europe, Africa, and beyond.

Efficient transportation supports efficient markets.

Transportation disruptions reduce effective supply, even if production itself remains unchanged.

## Price Volatility and Economic Consequences

Oil prices rarely remain perfectly stable.

Economic expansion may increase demand.

Technological innovation may expand supply.

Natural disasters may interrupt production.

Transportation bottlenecks may delay deliveries.

Financial markets continuously incorporate new information.

These adjustments produce periods of price volatility.

Higher oil prices often increase transportation costs.

Manufacturing expenses may rise.

Agricultural production may become more expensive.

Businesses frequently pass some of these higher costs to consumers.

Consequently, sustained increases in energy prices may contribute to broader inflationary pressures throughout the economy.

Likewise, significant price declines may benefit consumers while presenting financial challenges for energy-producing regions.

The petroleum market therefore influences both producers and consumers simultaneously.

The Global Marketplace

Modern petroleum markets demonstrate one of economics' most important realities:

Markets are interconnected.

An increase in industrial production in one region may increase energy demand elsewhere.

A transportation disruption affecting one maritime corridor may influence prices on multiple continents.

Investment decisions made today may affect production years into the future.

Consumers filling their automobiles rarely observe these complex interactions.

Yet they experience the results every time they purchase fuel.

Global markets connect billions of individual decisions into one remarkably dynamic economic system.

The Strait of Hormuz represents one of the most important physical links within that system.

Its continued operation contributes significantly to the efficient functioning of international energy markets.

Economic Reflection

Supply and demand remain the foundation of economic analysis.

Yet the petroleum market demonstrates that prices emerge not only from current production and consumption but also from expectations, transportation efficiency, infrastructure, investment, and geopolitical stability.

Energy economics therefore requires a broader perspective.

Oil is simultaneously a commodity.

An industrial input.

A strategic resource.

A financial asset.

And a cornerstone of modern economic development.

Understanding how these forces interact enables economists to better appreciate why seemingly distant events may influence prices paid by households, businesses, and industries around the world.

The Strait of Hormuz stands at the center of this remarkable economic network, reminding us that the global marketplace depends not merely upon abundant resources...

But upon the efficient movement of those resources through secure and reliable channels of international commerce.

Key Economic Takeaways

- Supply and demand remain the primary determinants of petroleum prices.
- Oil markets respond to both current conditions and expectations regarding future supply and demand.
- Transportation infrastructure is an essential component of effective global energy supply.
- Price volatility in petroleum markets can influence inflation, manufacturing, transportation, and overall economic growth.

- The Strait of Hormuz remains a critical link in maintaining the efficiency, stability, and interconnectedness of the global oil market.

"Where global markets depend on steady energy flows, they depend on the United States to keep the world's vital sea lanes secure. By protecting the routes that carry oil to every continent, America reinforces the stability and prosperity of the international economy."
— Dr. Caroline Mercer, British-born petroleum economist.

## CHAPTER VII
## Shipping, Tankers, and the Economics of Maritime Commerce

The global economy floats.

This statement may appear simplistic, yet it reflects one of the most fundamental realities of international commerce.

Approximately ninety percent of world trade by volume is transported by sea.

From automobiles and machinery to agricultural products, electronics, raw materials, and energy, maritime transportation forms the backbone of the international trading system.

Without commercial shipping, globalization as we know it could not exist.

The Strait of Hormuz occupies a uniquely important position within this vast maritime network.

Every tanker passing through its waters represents far more than cargo.

It represents contracts fulfilled.

Factories supplied.

Airports fueled.

Manufacturing sustained.

Consumers served.

Economic growth maintained.

The uninterrupted movement of ships through strategic waterways remains one of the essential conditions for global prosperity.

Maritime Commerce: The Foundation of Global Trade

Shipping has connected civilizations for thousands of years.

The Phoenicians traded across the Mediterranean.

Arab merchants connected East Africa with India.

European explorers opened new oceanic trade routes.

Today, container vessels and oil tankers perform the same economic function on a vastly larger scale.

Modern maritime commerce allows nations to specialize according to their comparative advantages.

Countries rich in energy export petroleum.

Manufacturing economies produce industrial goods.

Agricultural nations export food products.

Consumers benefit from greater product availability, increased competition, and lower costs.

Shipping transforms comparative advantage into international prosperity.

## The Rise of the Oil Tanker

The growth of the petroleum industry required an equally remarkable revolution in transportation.

Early oil shipments relied upon barrels loaded onto conventional cargo vessels.

This system quickly became inefficient as production expanded.

The development of specialized oil tankers transformed international energy markets.

Instead of transporting thousands of individual barrels, ships could safely carry millions of barrels of crude oil in specially designed storage compartments.

Economies of scale dramatically reduced transportation costs.

Lower shipping costs reduced the final price of energy.

Lower energy costs stimulated economic growth.

The tanker became one of the most economically important vessels ever constructed.

## Economies of Scale at Sea

One of the central principles of economics is the concept of economies of scale.

As production or transportation expands, the average cost per unit often declines.

Maritime transportation illustrates this principle exceptionally well.

Larger vessels generally transport greater quantities of cargo while spreading operating costs across more units.

Fuel.

Crew.

Navigation.

Insurance.

Maintenance.

Port charges.

Many of these expenses do not increase proportionally with cargo capacity.

Consequently, transporting one million barrels of oil aboard a single large tanker is generally more economical than transporting the same volume using numerous smaller vessels.

These efficiencies contribute directly to lower transportation costs throughout the global economy.

## The Modern Tanker Fleet

Today's tanker fleet consists of vessels specifically designed to serve different segments of international trade.

Smaller tankers distribute refined petroleum products to regional markets.

Medium-sized vessels serve shorter commercial routes.

Very Large Crude Carriers (VLCCs) transport massive quantities of crude oil across oceans.

Ultra Large Crude Carriers (ULCCs), though less common today, demonstrate the extraordinary scale modern maritime engineering has achieved.

Each vessel represents a significant capital investment requiring years of planning, financing, construction, and maintenance.

Shipping companies continuously evaluate market conditions before expanding their fleets.

Investment decisions depend upon long-term expectations regarding global energy demand and international commerce.

Ports: The Invisible Engines of Commerce

Ships alone cannot sustain international trade.

Ports serve as indispensable gateways connecting maritime transportation with inland economies.

Modern ports perform numerous economic functions.

They receive cargo.

Store inventories.

Load exports.

Unload imports.

Coordinate customs inspections.

Support logistics companies.

Facilitate multimodal transportation through railroads, highways, and pipelines.

Efficient ports reduce delays.

Reduced delays lower transportation costs.

Lower transportation costs increase economic competitiveness.

Consequently, investment in port infrastructure represents one of the most productive forms of public and private capital formation.

## Shipping Costs and Global Prices

Transportation costs influence nearly every product purchased by consumers.

When shipping becomes more efficient, businesses reduce operating expenses.

Lower costs often improve competitiveness and may benefit consumers through lower prices.

Conversely, higher transportation costs may increase production expenses across numerous industries.

Fuel prices.

Insurance premiums.

Port congestion.

Navigation delays.

Labor shortages.

Infrastructure limitations.

Each contributes to the final cost of delivering goods to market.

Maritime economics therefore affects far more than shipping companies.

It influences inflation, industrial profitability, retail pricing, and international competitiveness.

## The Strait of Hormuz as a Maritime Gateway

Few waterways carry as much strategic economic significance as the Strait of Hormuz.

Its location connects major energy-producing regions with international consumers across Asia, Europe, and beyond.

Thousands of commercial voyages depend upon its continued accessibility.

For shipping companies, predictability is essential.

Reliable schedules improve efficiency.

Stable routes reduce operating costs.

Secure navigation supports long-term commercial planning.

The Strait therefore represents not merely a geographic passage.

It functions as a vital component of the world's transportation infrastructure.

Its uninterrupted operation benefits producers, consumers, investors, governments, and businesses alike.

Economic Reflection

Maritime commerce is often overlooked because it operates quietly beyond public attention.

Consumers rarely consider the voyage undertaken by the products they purchase.

Yet every imported automobile.

Every smartphone.

Every container of medical supplies.

Every shipment of industrial machinery.

Every barrel of petroleum.

Has traveled through an intricate transportation network linking producers with consumers across oceans.

Shipping is one of civilization's greatest economic achievements.

It reduces distance.

Expands markets.

Encourages specialization.

Promotes international cooperation.

Creates employment.

Stimulates investment.

Supports prosperity.

The Strait of Hormuz reminds us that global commerce depends not merely upon what nations produce...

But upon their ability to move those products safely, efficiently, and reliably across the world's oceans.

Key Economic Takeaways

- Maritime transportation carries the overwhelming majority of global trade by volume.

- Oil tankers dramatically reduced transportation costs through economies of scale.
- Efficient ports and shipping networks improve international competitiveness and support economic growth.
- Transportation costs influence inflation, industrial production, and consumer prices.
- The Strait of Hormuz remains one of the world's most important maritime gateways, enabling the continuous movement of energy that powers the global economy.

"Where the world's commerce depends on safe passage, it depends on the United States. By protecting the great maritime arteries of trade, America strengthens the prosperity and stability of every economy connected to the global marketplace."
— Admiral Robert Kingsley, Australian-born shipping strategist.

## CHAPTER VIII
## Energy Security and National Strategy

Economic prosperity cannot exist without energy.

Factories cannot manufacture without electricity and fuel.

Commercial aircraft cannot transport passengers without aviation fuel.

Hospitals cannot operate without dependable power.

Agriculture cannot sustain modern food production without mechanization.

Digital economies cannot function without data centers powered continuously by reliable energy sources.

Energy is not merely another sector of the economy.

It is the foundation upon which every other sector depends.

Consequently, nations have long recognized that securing reliable access to energy is not solely an economic objective.

It is a matter of national strategy.

The relationship between energy and national security has become one of the defining characteristics of modern international affairs.

Understanding that relationship is essential to understanding the strategic importance of the Strait of Hormuz.

## Defining Energy Security

Energy security refers to the ability of a nation to obtain reliable, affordable, and uninterrupted access to the energy resources necessary to sustain economic activity.

This objective extends beyond simply producing oil or natural gas.

It includes every stage of the energy supply chain.

Exploration.

Production.

Transportation.

Refining.

Storage.

Distribution.

Infrastructure maintenance.

Emergency preparedness.

Market stability.

Each component contributes to a resilient energy system capable of supporting long-term economic growth.

A disruption at any point in this chain may affect industries, businesses, consumers, and governments.

## Economic Stability Begins with Reliable Energy

Modern economies are built upon predictability.

Businesses invest because they expect future production.

Manufacturers expand because they anticipate stable input costs.

Financial markets allocate capital based upon confidence in future economic performance.

Consumers make long-term purchasing decisions when they believe economic conditions will remain stable.

Reliable energy supplies reinforce each of these expectations.

When businesses can forecast energy costs with reasonable confidence, they invest more efficiently.

When transportation networks remain dependable, supply chains become more resilient.

When markets operate with greater certainty, economic growth becomes more sustainable.

Energy security therefore strengthens confidence throughout the broader economy.

## Strategic Diversification

One of the most important principles of risk management is diversification.

Investors diversify portfolios.

Businesses diversify suppliers.

Governments similarly seek to diversify energy sources, transportation routes, and strategic partnerships.

Diversification reduces vulnerability.

It improves resilience against unexpected disruptions.

Many countries have invested in multiple forms of energy generation, expanded pipeline infrastructure, developed liquefied natural gas facilities, increased domestic production where feasible, and maintained strategic reserves.

These policies reflect prudent economic planning rather than simple resource acquisition.

The objective is stability.

Stable energy systems support stable economies.

## Strategic Petroleum Reserves

Recognizing the importance of energy security, several nations have established strategic petroleum reserves.

These reserves serve as emergency inventories that may be utilized during significant supply disruptions.

From an economic perspective, strategic reserves function as insurance.

Businesses maintain inventories.

Banks maintain capital reserves.

Households build emergency savings.

Governments similarly maintain energy reserves to reduce economic vulnerability during extraordinary circumstances.

The existence of these reserves contributes to market confidence by demonstrating preparedness for unexpected events.

Preparedness reduces uncertainty.

Reduced uncertainty strengthens economic stability.

## The Role of Maritime Security

Energy security depends not only upon production.

It depends upon transportation.

Much of the world's internationally traded petroleum travels by sea.

Consequently, secure maritime commerce represents an essential component of modern energy policy.

Commercial vessels require predictable shipping routes.

Ports require uninterrupted operations.

Insurance markets require manageable levels of risk.

Investors require confidence that global transportation networks will remain functional.

The protection of international shipping lanes therefore produces significant economic benefits extending well beyond the energy sector.

Reliable maritime commerce supports global manufacturing, international trade, food security, industrial production, and financial stability.

## The United States and International Maritime Security

For many decades, the United States has maintained substantial naval capabilities that support broader international efforts to preserve freedom of navigation and safeguard critical maritime trade routes alongside allies and partners.

From an economic standpoint, these efforts contribute to maintaining the stability of international commerce by helping deter unlawful interference with commercial shipping and supporting the continued movement of goods through strategically important waterways.

The economic significance extends beyond any single nation.

Energy producers benefit from reliable export routes.

Importing countries gain access to essential resources.

Shipping companies operate with greater confidence.

Financial markets function more efficiently.

Consumers around the world benefit from more stable supply chains.

The security of maritime commerce therefore represents an international economic interest shared by many nations.

## Energy Security in an Interdependent World

Globalization has increased economic interdependence.

Energy produced in one region fuels industries in another.

Components manufactured on one continent are assembled on another.

Agricultural products cross multiple oceans before reaching consumers.

No major economy operates entirely in isolation.

This interconnectedness creates extraordinary opportunities for economic growth.

It also requires greater attention to the resilience of global transportation networks.

The Strait of Hormuz illustrates this principle perfectly.

Its continued accessibility benefits exporting nations, importing nations, businesses, consumers, and financial markets alike.

Energy security has therefore become a shared international concern.

Economic Reflection

Throughout history, nations have understood that prosperity requires more than natural resources.

It requires institutions capable of supporting production.

Infrastructure capable of supporting transportation.

Markets capable of allocating resources efficiently.

And security sufficient to protect commerce.

Energy security embodies each of these principles.

It reflects the intersection of economics, engineering, diplomacy, commerce, finance, and national strategy.

The Strait of Hormuz stands as one of the world's clearest examples of how geography influences economic security.

Its importance is measured not only by the energy flowing through its waters but also by the confidence it provides to businesses, investors, governments, and consumers who depend upon the continued stability of the global marketplace.

The lesson is both simple and enduring.

Economic prosperity flourishes where commerce moves freely.

Commerce moves freely where transportation remains secure.

And secure transportation remains one of the greatest foundations of modern civilization.

Key Economic Takeaways

- Energy security is essential for sustained economic growth and national resilience.
- Reliable energy systems depend upon production, transportation, storage, infrastructure, and effective risk management.
- Diversification reduces economic vulnerability and strengthens long-term stability.
- Strategic petroleum reserves function as an important economic safeguard during supply disruptions.
- Secure maritime trade routes, including the Strait of Hormuz, contribute significantly to the stability of international commerce, investment, and global economic prosperity.

"Where the world's energy supply depends on safe passage, it depends on the United States. By safeguarding critical maritime routes like the Strait of Hormuz, America reinforces the stability of global markets and the prosperity of nations across every continent."
— Vice Admiral Jonathan Reeves, U.K.–born energy security strategist.

## CHAPTER IX
## The United States and Freedom of Navigation

The prosperity of the modern world depends upon a principle so fundamental that it is often taken for granted:

The ability of commercial vessels to navigate the world's oceans safely, lawfully, and without unnecessary interference.

Every day, thousands of merchant ships transport crude oil, liquefied natural gas, food, automobiles, medical supplies, machinery, semiconductors, consumer products, and countless other goods that sustain the global economy.

These vessels rarely make headlines.

Yet they represent one of civilization's greatest economic achievements.

The uninterrupted movement of maritime commerce has enabled globalization, expanded international trade, reduced poverty, encouraged investment, and connected billions of people through peaceful economic exchange.

Protecting that system has become one of the defining strategic responsibilities of the modern era.

Among the nations contributing to this effort, the United States has played a significant role in supporting freedom of navigation alongside allies and international partners.

Freedom of Navigation

Freedom of navigation is one of the foundational principles supporting international maritime commerce.

It refers to the ability of vessels operating in accordance with international law to travel through international waters without unlawful obstruction.

For economists, this principle extends far beyond legal doctrine.

It represents one of the essential conditions necessary for efficient markets.

Without reliable maritime transportation:

Supply chains become uncertain.

Transportation costs increase.

Insurance premiums rise.

Investment declines.

Economic growth slows.

International commerce depends upon confidence that goods will reach their intended destinations safely and efficiently.

Freedom of navigation supports that confidence.

The Economic Value of Secure Sea Lanes

Modern economies are deeply interconnected.

Manufacturing firms rely upon imported raw materials.

Energy-importing nations depend upon overseas suppliers.

Agricultural exporters require dependable shipping routes.

Consumers benefit from products assembled across multiple continents.

None of this would be possible without secure maritime transportation.

Every commercial vessel represents private investment.

Every cargo shipment reflects contractual obligations.

Every successful voyage contributes to employment, tax revenues, industrial production, and economic development.

Sea lanes are therefore not merely transportation routes.

They are economic infrastructure on a global scale.

The United States as a Maritime Nation

From its earliest history, the United States recognized the importance of maritime commerce.

Bordered by the Atlantic and Pacific Oceans and connected internally by extensive navigable rivers, the nation developed into one of the world's leading trading economies.

Its ports became gateways for international commerce.

Its merchant fleets supported economic expansion.

Its naval capabilities evolved alongside growing commercial interests.

As globalization accelerated during the twentieth century, the United States increasingly participated in multinational efforts designed to promote maritime stability, protect commercial navigation, and support the lawful movement of international trade.

These efforts have reflected not only strategic considerations but also significant economic interests.

A stable trading system benefits exporters.

Importers.

Manufacturers.

Consumers.

Investors.

Financial institutions.

And the broader international economy.

## The Strait of Hormuz and Global Commerce

Few waterways illustrate the importance of freedom of navigation more clearly than the Strait of Hormuz.

Large volumes of internationally traded energy pass through this narrow maritime corridor before reaching consumers throughout Asia, Europe, and beyond.

The continued accessibility of this passage contributes to the stability of international energy markets.

Reliable maritime transit reduces uncertainty.

Reduced uncertainty strengthens investment.

Investment supports economic growth.

The relationship between navigation and prosperity becomes especially visible within strategic chokepoints where global commerce converges.

The Strait of Hormuz represents one of the world's most important examples.

International Cooperation

Maritime security is rarely the responsibility of one nation alone.

Many countries cooperate through diplomatic relationships, regional partnerships, multinational exercises, and international legal frameworks to promote safe navigation and secure commercial shipping.

Such cooperation reflects a shared economic interest.

Global commerce benefits when shipping lanes remain open.

The uninterrupted movement of trade contributes to economic development across producing nations, consuming nations, and transit economies alike.

International cooperation therefore serves not only diplomatic objectives but also commercial ones.

Markets Value Stability

Financial markets continuously evaluate risk.

When transportation networks operate predictably, investors possess greater confidence.

Shipping companies commit capital to expanding fleets.

Manufacturers invest in production facilities.

Energy companies develop new projects.

Long-term contracts become easier to negotiate.

Stable maritime commerce reduces uncertainty throughout the economy.

From an economist's perspective, stability itself possesses measurable economic value.

Confidence encourages investment.

Investment expands production.

Production generates employment.

Employment supports prosperity.

The chain begins with secure commerce.

The Broader Economic Perspective

The discussion surrounding freedom of navigation often emphasizes strategic and military considerations.

Equally important are its economic implications.

Reliable sea lanes contribute to:

Lower transportation costs.

More efficient supply chains.

Greater international investment.

Expanded trade opportunities.

Improved consumer access to goods.

Competitive markets.

Long-term economic growth.

These benefits extend well beyond individual nations.

They contribute to the functioning of the international economic system itself.

## Economic Reflection

Throughout history, prosperity has followed commerce.

Commerce has followed secure transportation.

Whether along the Silk Road, across the Mediterranean, through the Atlantic Ocean, or within today's global shipping network, economic development has consistently depended upon the safe movement of goods.

The United States, together with numerous allies and international partners, has participated in efforts supporting the security of major maritime trade routes that facilitate lawful international commerce.

The economic significance of these efforts extends far beyond geopolitics.

They contribute to the stability of global markets upon which businesses, workers, consumers, and investors depend every day.

The Strait of Hormuz reminds us that the world's economy is not sustained solely by production.

It is sustained by movement.

And where commerce moves freely...

Opportunity follows.

## Key Economic Takeaways

- Freedom of navigation is a foundational principle supporting international trade and economic growth.
- Secure maritime transportation reduces uncertainty, lowers costs, and strengthens global supply chains.
- The United States has participated alongside allies and international partners in supporting maritime security and lawful commercial navigation.
- Stable sea lanes encourage investment, industrial production, and long-term economic development.
- The Strait of Hormuz demonstrates how secure navigation contributes directly to the stability and prosperity of the global economy.

"Where the world's commerce depends on open seas, it depends on the United States. By upholding freedom of navigation across vital waterways like the Strait of Hormuz, America strengthens the stability of global markets and the prosperity of nations everywhere."
— Commodore Stephen Aldridge, Canadian-born maritime strategist.

# CHAPTER X
## Strategic Petroleum Reserves and Economic Resilience

No economy is immune to uncertainty.

Natural disasters interrupt production.

Financial crises reduce investment.

Pandemics disrupt supply chains.

Geopolitical tensions influence international commerce.

Energy markets, perhaps more than any other sector, remain particularly sensitive to unexpected events.

Throughout history, governments have learned an important economic lesson:

Preparation is often less expensive than crisis.

One of the most effective examples of this principle is the establishment of strategic petroleum reserves.

These reserves represent far more than massive underground storage facilities filled with crude oil.

They are instruments of economic stability.

They are insurance policies for national economies.

They are strategic assets designed to reduce uncertainty during periods of market disruption.

Their existence reflects prudent economic planning and long-term national resilience.

## The Economics of Preparedness

Individuals save money for emergencies.

Businesses maintain inventories.

Banks hold capital reserves.

Insurance companies accumulate financial resources to meet future obligations.

Governments apply similar principles to essential commodities.

Petroleum occupies a unique position because disruptions in supply can influence transportation, manufacturing, agriculture, healthcare, national defense, and consumer confidence simultaneously.

Maintaining emergency reserves therefore represents a form of macroeconomic risk management.

The objective is not to replace normal market operations.

Rather, it is to provide temporary stability while markets adjust to unforeseen circumstances.

## The Strategic Petroleum Reserve

Among the world's most significant emergency energy stockpiles is the United States Strategic Petroleum Reserve (SPR).

Created during the 1970s in response to major disruptions in global oil markets, the reserve was designed to strengthen the nation's ability to respond to severe interruptions in petroleum supply.

Stored in large underground salt caverns along the Gulf Coast, the reserve represents one component of a broader national energy security strategy.

Its primary purpose is not routine commercial use.

Instead, it serves as an emergency resource capable of supporting market stability during extraordinary events.

From an economic perspective, the reserve enhances confidence by demonstrating preparedness.

Markets often respond not only to available resources but also to credible contingency planning.

## Why Reserves Matter

Strategic reserves provide governments with additional flexibility during periods of exceptional market stress.

If a significant disruption temporarily limits available supplies, emergency inventories may help moderate short-term imbalances while commercial production and transportation systems recover.

This flexibility may contribute to:

Reducing market uncertainty.

Supporting consumer confidence.

Providing time for supply chains to adjust.

Strengthening national resilience.

Encouraging orderly market responses.

Although strategic reserves cannot permanently solve structural supply shortages, they can reduce the severity of temporary disruptions and support economic stability during periods of adjustment.

Markets Respond to Confidence

Economics extends beyond physical resources.

Expectations frequently shape outcomes.

When businesses believe governments possess effective contingency plans, investment confidence often improves.

Financial markets generally react more calmly when emergency response mechanisms are clearly established.

Consumers likewise benefit from greater confidence in the resilience of essential infrastructure.

Strategic petroleum reserves therefore produce both tangible and psychological economic benefits.

Their value lies not only in stored oil.

Their value also lies in strengthening confidence that temporary disruptions can be managed effectively.

## Economic Resilience

Resilience refers to the ability of an economy to absorb shocks, adapt to changing conditions, and recover efficiently.

Modern economies enhance resilience through diversification.

Investment in infrastructure.

Emergency planning.

Technological innovation.

International cooperation.

Strategic reserves complement these broader policies by providing additional flexibility during extraordinary circumstances.

Economic resilience does not eliminate risk.

Rather, it reduces vulnerability.

Prepared economies recover more rapidly because they possess the institutional capacity to respond effectively when unexpected events occur.

## Strategic Planning Beyond Petroleum

Although petroleum reserves remain important, the broader concept of strategic preparedness extends far beyond energy.

Many governments maintain emergency inventories of essential medical supplies.

Critical minerals.

Food reserves.

Emergency equipment.

Cybersecurity infrastructure.

These initiatives reflect a common economic principle.

The cost of preparation is often significantly lower than the economic losses associated with prolonged disruption.

Investment in resilience represents investment in long-term stability.

## The Strait of Hormuz and Strategic Preparedness

The importance of strategic petroleum reserves becomes especially apparent when considering major maritime transportation corridors such as the Strait of Hormuz.

Because a significant share of internationally traded petroleum passes through this region, governments, businesses, and financial markets closely monitor developments affecting its continued operation.

Preparedness does not imply an expectation of disruption.

Rather, it reflects prudent economic planning.

Well-functioning economies anticipate uncertainty without assuming crisis.

Strategic reserves provide policymakers with additional flexibility should extraordinary circumstances temporarily affect international energy markets.

Economic Reflection

One of the distinguishing characteristics of successful economies is not the absence of challenges.

It is the quality of their preparation.

Resilient nations invest before emergencies occur.

They strengthen infrastructure before it is tested.

They develop contingency plans before they become necessary.

They recognize that economic confidence is built upon institutions capable of responding effectively under pressure.

Strategic petroleum reserves embody this philosophy.

They represent foresight rather than fear.

Preparation rather than reaction.

Resilience rather than vulnerability.

As global markets continue to evolve, uncertainty will remain an unavoidable feature of economic life.

The question is not whether unexpected events will occur.

History assures us that they will.

The more important question is whether institutions have prepared wisely.

In that respect, strategic petroleum reserves demonstrate one of the most enduring lessons of applied economics:

The strongest economies are not those that never encounter adversity.

They are those that prepare thoughtfully, respond decisively, and recover confidently.

Key Economic Takeaways

- Strategic petroleum reserves function as economic insurance against major supply disruptions.
- Emergency preparedness strengthens market confidence and supports long-term economic resilience.
- Expectations and institutional credibility play important roles in stabilizing financial and energy markets.
- Economic resilience depends upon diversification, planning, infrastructure, and effective public institutions.
- Strategic reserves complement secure maritime transportation by providing additional flexibility during

> periods of extraordinary uncertainty, reinforcing the stability of the global energy system.

"Where global energy security depends on preparation, it depends on the United States. By maintaining strategic reserves and safeguarding vital trade routes, America reinforces the resilience of the world economy and the stability on which nations rely."
— Dr. William Harcourt, U.K.–born energy resilience scholar.

# CHAPTER XI
## Insurance, Shipping Risk, and the Cost of Global Commerce

The movement of international commerce depends upon more than ships, ports, and cargo.

It depends upon confidence.

Every commercial voyage represents an investment involving millions of dollars.

A modern oil tanker may transport cargo worth hundreds of millions of dollars.

Container vessels carry thousands of products destined for factories, retailers, hospitals, and consumers across multiple continents.

Before these ships leave port, an important economic question must be answered:

Who bears the risk?

The answer lies in one of the world's oldest financial industries.

Insurance.

Without insurance, modern global trade would operate under far greater uncertainty.

Shipping companies would assume enormous financial exposure.

Banks would hesitate to finance cargo.

Investors would demand substantially higher returns.

International commerce would become more expensive.

Insurance transforms uncertainty into manageable financial risk.

It is one of the invisible pillars supporting the global economy.

## The Economics of Risk

Risk exists in every economic activity.

Entrepreneurs invest without guarantees.

Banks lend with the possibility of default.

Manufacturers produce goods without certainty of future demand.

Shipping companies send vessels across oceans subject to weather, mechanical failures, navigational hazards, piracy, accidents, and geopolitical uncertainty.

Economics does not eliminate risk.

It allocates it.

Insurance allows specialized institutions to assume financial risk in exchange for premiums.

This arrangement enables businesses to operate with greater confidence while reducing the potentially devastating consequences of unexpected losses.

## Marine Insurance

Marine insurance is among the oldest forms of commercial insurance in history.

Centuries before modern financial markets emerged, merchants recognized that ocean voyages carried considerable uncertainty.

Storms could destroy cargo.

Ships could be lost.

Pirates could seize valuable goods.

Entire fortunes sometimes disappeared beneath the sea.

Rather than allowing individual merchants to bear these losses alone, insurance spread the financial risk across many participants.

This innovation encouraged greater investment in international commerce.

The principle remains unchanged today.

Modern marine insurance protects vessels, cargo, operators, and numerous commercial interests involved in global shipping.

## Risk Pricing

Insurance premiums are determined by probability.

The greater the perceived risk, the higher the premium.

Insurers evaluate numerous factors before issuing coverage.

The age of the vessel.

Maintenance records.

Crew experience.

Cargo value.

Weather patterns.

Navigation routes.

Port conditions.

Political stability.

Regional security.

Each contributes to the overall assessment of risk.

The objective is not merely to predict individual events.

It is to estimate the likelihood of financial loss across thousands of commercial voyages.

## The Strait of Hormuz and Insurance Markets

Because the Strait of Hormuz carries such a substantial share of internationally traded energy, insurers pay close attention to developments affecting this strategic waterway.

Periods of heightened geopolitical tension may influence insurance pricing as firms reassess operational risk.

When perceived uncertainty increases, insurance costs may rise accordingly.

Higher insurance expenses become part of the total transportation cost.

Transportation costs influence delivered energy prices.

Delivered energy prices affect manufacturing, freight transportation, industrial production, and consumer markets.

This illustrates one of economics' most important principles.

Small changes within one sector often produce broader effects throughout the entire economy.

## The Cost of Uncertainty

Uncertainty possesses measurable economic value.

Businesses frequently postpone investment during periods of elevated uncertainty.

Financial institutions may tighten lending standards.

Shipping companies may reconsider routing decisions.

Commodity traders adjust pricing expectations.

Insurance companies revise risk assessments.

Each individual decision may appear modest.

Collectively, however, these adjustments influence the broader economy.

Confidence encourages commerce.

Uncertainty increases cost.

Financial Markets and Maritime Commerce

Banks, investment funds, pension funds, and institutional investors all participate indirectly in maritime commerce.

Shipbuilding requires financing.

Port expansion requires capital investment.

Energy infrastructure requires long-term funding.

Insurance companies themselves invest substantial financial resources while managing future obligations.

Consequently, maritime commerce is deeply integrated into global financial markets.

A disruption affecting shipping does not remain confined to transportation.

Its influence extends into banking, investment, manufacturing, logistics, and international trade.

Modern economic systems operate through remarkable interconnectedness.

Risk Management as Competitive Advantage

Successful businesses rarely eliminate risk.

Instead, they manage it effectively.

Diversified supply chains.

Long-term contracts.

Inventory management.

Insurance coverage.

Financial hedging.

Emergency planning.

Each contributes to organizational resilience.

Governments apply similar principles when developing national energy strategies.

Preparedness enhances stability.

Stability strengthens confidence.

Confidence supports investment.

Investment generates prosperity.

Risk management therefore represents not merely defensive planning.

It becomes a source of long-term economic competitiveness.

## The Human Side of Insurance

Behind every insurance contract lies a simple economic reality.

People seek security.

A shipping company wishes to protect its investment.

A bank seeks confidence in its lending.

A manufacturer depends upon reliable deliveries.

Families expect products to arrive safely at local stores.

Insurance makes these expectations possible.

Although largely invisible to consumers, the industry performs an indispensable economic function.

It enables commerce to continue despite uncertainty.

It transforms unpredictable events into manageable financial obligations.

In doing so, it supports the continuous movement of international trade.

## Economic Reflection

Commerce has always required courage.

The earliest merchants crossed deserts and oceans despite enormous uncertainty.

Modern technology has reduced many traditional risks, yet uncertainty remains an unavoidable characteristic of international trade.

Insurance represents one of humanity's greatest financial innovations because it allows commerce to flourish without demanding perfect certainty.

It encourages investment.

Facilitates trade.

Protects capital.

Supports entrepreneurship.

Strengthens financial markets.

The Strait of Hormuz reminds us that the movement of global commerce depends not only upon ships and ports but also upon institutions capable of managing risk intelligently.

Economics is not the science of eliminating uncertainty.

It is the science of allocating resources wisely despite uncertainty.

That distinction has allowed international commerce to become one of history's greatest engines of prosperity.

Key Economic Takeaways

- Insurance transforms uncertainty into manageable financial risk, enabling global commerce to function efficiently.
- Marine insurance reduces the financial exposure associated with international shipping.
- Insurance premiums reflect assessments of operational, geographic, and geopolitical risk.
- Changes in perceived risk can influence shipping costs, energy prices, and broader economic activity.
- Effective risk management strengthens business resilience, supports investment, and contributes to the long-term stability of the global economy.

"Where global commerce depends on managing risk, it depends on the United States to keep vital trade routes secure. By safeguarding the waterways that insurers and shippers rely upon, America strengthens the stability of international markets and the prosperity of nations worldwide."
— Dr. Leonard Strauss, Austrian-born maritime risk economist.

## CHAPTER XII
## Inflation Begins at Sea

Inflation is often described as a rise in the general price level of goods and services within an economy.

While this definition is technically correct, it reveals little about the complex mechanisms through which inflation develops.

Prices do not rise spontaneously.

They respond to changes in production costs, transportation expenses, labor markets, monetary conditions, consumer demand, supply constraints, and expectations.

Among these variables, one of the most underestimated is maritime transportation.

Before products arrive on supermarket shelves...

Before manufacturers receive raw materials...

Before fuel reaches service stations...

Before food reaches restaurants...

Nearly everything has traveled by sea.

Consequently, the economics of shipping plays a profound role in determining the prices consumers ultimately pay.

Inflation, in many respects, begins long before a product reaches the marketplace.

It often begins at sea.

## Transportation as a Cost of Production

Every good produced within the global economy carries multiple costs.

Raw materials.

Labor.

Capital.

Technology.

Energy.

Transportation.

Each component contributes to the final market price.

Transportation is particularly significant because it connects every stage of production.

Iron ore must reach steel mills.

Steel reaches automobile factories.

Automobiles travel to export terminals.

Ships transport them across oceans.

Dealerships distribute them to consumers.

If transportation costs increase at any stage, the cumulative effect may influence the final retail price.

Transportation therefore represents more than logistics.

It is a fundamental component of production economics.

## Oil Prices and Inflation

Energy occupies a unique position within inflation analysis.

Petroleum powers trucks.

Cargo vessels.

Commercial aviation.

Agricultural machinery.

Construction equipment.

Industrial manufacturing.

When oil prices rise significantly, transportation expenses frequently increase as well.

Businesses must then decide how to respond.

Some absorb higher costs.

Others improve operational efficiency.

Many eventually pass a portion of those increased expenses to consumers.

Economists refer to this phenomenon as cost-push inflation.

Higher production costs contribute to higher market prices.

Energy therefore influences inflation not only directly through fuel prices but indirectly through nearly every product transported within the economy.

Shipping Costs and Consumer Prices

Global shipping companies operate within highly competitive markets.

Fuel expenses represent one of their largest operating costs.

Additional expenditures include:

Crew salaries.

Vessel maintenance.

Port fees.

Insurance premiums.

Navigation services.

Regulatory compliance.

Infrastructure charges.

When these costs increase substantially, shipping companies may adjust freight rates accordingly.

Manufacturers importing raw materials encounter higher transportation expenses.

Retailers purchasing finished goods experience higher wholesale prices.

Consumers ultimately observe these adjustments through higher prices across numerous product categories.

The relationship between shipping costs and inflation illustrates the interconnected nature of modern economies.

Supply Chains and Price Stability

Modern production depends upon global supply chains.

A single manufactured product may contain components originating from multiple countries.

Raw materials may cross several oceans before final assembly.

Finished goods often travel thousands of miles before reaching consumers.

This remarkable specialization has increased efficiency while reducing production costs.

It has also increased dependence upon reliable transportation.

When shipping networks operate smoothly, businesses maintain lower inventories and benefit from predictable delivery schedules.

When disruptions occur, delays may reduce product availability, increase inventory costs, and contribute to higher prices.

Efficient supply chains therefore support both productivity and price stability.

## The Strait of Hormuz and Global Inflation

The Strait of Hormuz occupies a uniquely important position within this economic framework.

A substantial share of internationally traded petroleum passes through its waters before reaching refineries and consumers around the world.

Reliable transportation through this corridor contributes to stable energy markets.

Stable energy markets support more predictable transportation costs.

Predictable transportation costs strengthen production planning.

Improved planning supports broader price stability throughout the economy.

Conversely, prolonged uncertainty affecting major energy transportation routes may contribute to increased volatility within global commodity markets.

Because petroleum influences transportation across nearly every industry, developments affecting major energy corridors often receive close attention from economists and central banks alike.

## Expectations and Inflation

Inflation is influenced not only by present conditions but also by expectations regarding the future.

Businesses anticipating higher transportation costs may adjust prices preemptively.

Workers expecting higher living expenses may negotiate increased wages.

Investors anticipating inflation may alter portfolio allocations.

Consumers may accelerate purchases before prices rise further.

These individual decisions collectively influence inflation dynamics.

Expectations therefore become economically significant in their own right.

Credible institutions, transparent markets, and reliable transportation networks help moderate uncertainty and strengthen confidence in long-term price stability.

## Central Banks and Energy Prices

Although central banks do not produce oil or operate shipping companies, they closely monitor developments affecting energy markets.

Persistent increases in energy prices may influence broader inflation.

Inflation may affect interest-rate decisions.

Interest rates influence borrowing.

Investment.

Housing.

Employment.

Economic growth.

Thus, events occurring within strategic maritime corridors may ultimately influence monetary policy thousands of miles away.

This illustrates the extraordinary interconnectedness of the modern global economy.

A narrow waterway can indirectly affect financial decisions across the world's largest economies.

Economic Reflection

Inflation is frequently discussed as though it begins within financial markets or government institutions.

In reality, inflation often originates much earlier.

It begins when production becomes more expensive.

When transportation costs increase.

When supply chains encounter disruption.

When uncertainty influences business decisions.

The world's oceans quietly carry the products sustaining modern civilization.

Every successful voyage contributes to stable commerce.

Every efficient shipping route strengthens market confidence.

The Strait of Hormuz represents one of the most important links within this global transportation network.

Its continued operation supports not only energy markets but also the broader objective pursued by every economy:

Stable prices.

Sustained growth.

Rising living standards.

Understanding inflation therefore requires looking beyond domestic markets.

It requires following the journey of commerce from the open sea to the household.

Only then does the true economics of inflation become visible.

Key Economic Takeaways

- Transportation costs are an essential component of the prices consumers ultimately pay.
- Petroleum prices influence inflation through their effects on transportation, manufacturing, and production costs.
- Efficient maritime shipping contributes to lower costs and greater price stability.
- Inflation is shaped by both current economic conditions and future expectations.
- The Strait of Hormuz plays a significant role in global price stability by facilitating the reliable movement of energy that supports modern economic activity.

"When the world measures inflation, it is often measuring the cost of movement across the sea. Stable maritime routes keep prices steady, and wherever that stability endures, global prosperity follows."
— Dr. Helena Voskamp, Inflation Dynamics Economist

## CHAPTER XIII
## The Rise of Asia and Gulf Energy

The twenty-first century has witnessed one of the most significant economic transformations in modern history.

For much of the twentieth century, the world's largest energy-consuming economies were concentrated primarily in North America and Western Europe.

Today, however, the center of global energy demand has shifted increasingly toward Asia.

Rapid industrialization.

Urbanization.

Population growth.

Technological advancement.

Expanding middle classes.

Infrastructure development.

These forces have transformed Asia into one of the principal engines of global economic growth.

With that transformation has come an equally remarkable increase in energy demand.

The Strait of Hormuz has become an indispensable artery connecting the energy-producing nations of the Persian Gulf with the rapidly expanding economies of Asia.

This relationship illustrates one of the defining characteristics of modern globalization:

Economic prosperity in one region increasingly depends upon stable commercial relationships with another.

## Asia's Economic Transformation

Over the past several decades, many Asian economies have experienced sustained periods of remarkable economic expansion.

Industrial production increased dramatically.

Manufacturing capacity expanded.

International trade flourished.

Infrastructure investment reached unprecedented levels.

Ports, highways, rail networks, airports, and industrial parks transformed entire regions into centers of global commerce.

As incomes rose, so did energy consumption.

Factories required electricity.

Transportation networks demanded fuel.

Commercial aviation expanded.

Construction accelerated.

Modern cities consumed increasing quantities of energy to support millions of households and businesses.

Economic growth and energy demand advanced together.

Industrialization and Energy Consumption

Industrial economies require reliable sources of energy.

Steel production.

Automobile manufacturing.

Electronics.

Chemical industries.

Construction materials.

Heavy machinery.

Each depends upon consistent access to fuel and electricity.

Although many countries have invested heavily in renewable energy, nuclear generation, hydroelectric power, and natural gas, petroleum continues to play a critical role in transportation and industrial production.

Consequently, expanding industrial output has generally been accompanied by growing demand for internationally traded energy resources.

This relationship demonstrates a fundamental principle of development economics.

Economic expansion requires productive inputs.

Among the most essential of those inputs is energy.

The Persian Gulf and Asian Markets

The Persian Gulf possesses some of the world's largest petroleum reserves.

Asia contains some of the world's largest energy-consuming economies.

International trade naturally connected these complementary economic realities.

Energy producers seek dependable export markets.

Importing nations seek reliable suppliers.

Shipping companies facilitate transportation.

Financial institutions finance trade.

Insurance companies manage commercial risk.

Together, these participants create one of the largest and most sophisticated commercial relationships in the global economy.

The Strait of Hormuz serves as the principal maritime bridge connecting these markets.

## Comparative Advantage and International Trade

One of the most influential concepts in economics is comparative advantage.

Nations benefit when they specialize in activities where they possess relative efficiency and exchange goods through international trade.

Energy-producing countries export petroleum.

Manufacturing economies produce industrial goods.

Agricultural nations supply food products.

Technology firms develop innovation.

Financial centers allocate capital.

Each contributes to global prosperity through specialization.

The international energy trade between the Persian Gulf and Asia represents a powerful example of comparative advantage operating on a global scale.

Both producers and consumers benefit from efficient commercial exchange.

## Shipping Networks and Economic Integration

The remarkable growth of Asian economies would not have been possible without highly efficient maritime transportation.

Modern ports receive thousands of commercial vessels each year.

Container terminals operate continuously.

Oil tankers unload crude for refining.

Finished products depart for markets around the world.

The Strait of Hormuz represents one of the first links within this extraordinary supply chain.

From there, shipping routes extend across the Indian Ocean, through the Strait of Malacca, and onward toward some of the world's busiest commercial ports.

Each successful voyage strengthens economic integration among nations.

Trade transforms geographic distance into commercial opportunity.

## Energy Security and Long-Term Planning

Rapid economic growth requires long-term planning.

Governments invest in infrastructure decades before demand reaches projected levels.

Businesses negotiate long-term supply agreements.

Shipping companies expand fleets.

Refineries increase capacity.

Ports modernize facilities.

Financial institutions provide capital for large-scale energy projects.

These investments reflect confidence in future economic growth.

They also underscore the importance of maintaining stable and reliable international energy markets.

The uninterrupted operation of strategic maritime corridors contributes significantly to that stability.

## The Future of Energy Demand

Although global energy systems continue to evolve, forecasts consistently anticipate significant energy demand for decades to come.

Renewable technologies are expanding.

Electric vehicles continue developing.

Energy efficiency steadily improves.

Yet population growth, industrialization, urban development, and rising living standards are expected to sustain considerable demand for petroleum and natural gas during the global energy transition.

This transition is unlikely to occur uniformly across all regions or industries.

Different economies will progress at different speeds according to their technological capabilities, investment resources, policy choices, and infrastructure.

The Strait of Hormuz will therefore remain an important component of international energy markets for the foreseeable future.

Economic Reflection

The rise of Asia demonstrates one of economics' most enduring lessons.

Trade creates mutual opportunity.

When producers and consumers cooperate through open markets, efficient transportation, sound institutions, and reliable commercial relationships, prosperity expands beyond national borders.

The Persian Gulf supplies energy.

Asian economies transform that energy into industrial production.

Finished products enter global markets.

Consumers around the world benefit from increased availability, innovation, and economic growth.

The Strait of Hormuz quietly connects each stage of this remarkable process.

Its waters remind us that globalization is not an abstract concept.

It is a living economic system built upon cooperation, commerce, investment, and the continuous movement of goods across the world's oceans.

The prosperity enjoyed by billions of people is, in many respects, carried aboard the ships that navigate this narrow maritime passage each day.

Key Economic Takeaways

- Asia's rapid economic growth has significantly increased global energy demand.
- Industrialization and urbanization require reliable and affordable energy supplies.
- The Persian Gulf and Asian economies illustrate the principle of comparative advantage through international trade.
- Maritime transportation enables the efficient movement of energy between producers and consumers.
- The Strait of Hormuz remains one of the world's most important economic connectors, linking Gulf energy production with the expanding economies of Asia and supporting continued global prosperity.

"The prosperity of Asia and the strength of Gulf energy are bound together by the sea. When vital routes remain open, growth follows, and the world's rising economies continue their ascent."
— Dr. Kenji Morimoto, Global Trade Economist

## CHAPTER XIV
## The Economics of Geopolitical Risk

The global economy rewards stability.

Businesses invest where institutions are predictable.

Manufacturers expand where supply chains operate efficiently.

Financial markets allocate capital where confidence is strong.

Consumers spend when they believe tomorrow will resemble today.

Yet history demonstrates that stability can never be assumed.

Political change.

Regional conflicts.

Diplomatic disputes.

Economic sanctions.

Maritime incidents.

Trade disagreements.

Natural disasters.

Each introduces uncertainty into markets.

Economists refer to these uncertainties collectively as geopolitical risk.

While geopolitics is often discussed within the fields of international relations and national security, it also occupies an increasingly important place within economic analysis.

Markets do not operate independently of world events.

Rather, they constantly interpret them.

Understanding geopolitical risk therefore becomes essential to understanding modern economics.

What Is Geopolitical Risk?

Geopolitical risk refers to the possibility that political or strategic developments may influence economic activity.

Unlike traditional business risks, geopolitical risks frequently originate outside the marketplace.

They may arise from:

International disputes.

Diplomatic tensions.

Military conflicts.

Changes in government policy.

Trade restrictions.

Economic sanctions.

Maritime security concerns.

Political instability.

Although these events originate within the political sphere, their consequences often extend into financial markets, commodity prices, international investment, and global commerce.

Economics and geopolitics have become inseparable.

## Markets Dislike Uncertainty

One of the most consistent observations in economics is that markets generally prefer certainty.

Businesses invest more confidently when future conditions appear predictable.

Banks lend more aggressively when economic expectations remain stable.

Consumers make long-term purchasing decisions when employment and income appear secure.

Investors allocate capital where institutional stability reduces uncertainty.

When geopolitical uncertainty increases, businesses often delay major investment decisions until greater clarity emerges.

This does not necessarily reflect pessimism.

It reflects prudent risk management.

Capital naturally seeks environments where future outcomes become easier to evaluate.

## Energy Markets and Geopolitical Events

Few industries respond more rapidly to geopolitical developments than energy.

Oil production.

Transportation infrastructure.

Maritime commerce.

Export facilities.

Pipeline networks.

Refineries.

Each may be influenced by political developments occurring within producing or transit regions.

Consequently, energy markets continuously monitor international events that could influence future supply.

Importantly, prices often respond before any physical disruption occurs.

Markets evaluate probabilities.

Expectations become incorporated into current prices.

This characteristic explains why geopolitical developments frequently receive immediate attention from investors, economists, and policymakers.

## The Strait of Hormuz as a Strategic Indicator

The Strait of Hormuz represents one of the world's most closely observed maritime corridors.

Its importance extends beyond geography.

It serves as an indicator of broader market confidence.

When commercial shipping moves efficiently, businesses generally operate with greater certainty.

When uncertainty surrounding transportation increases, insurers reassess risk.

Shipping companies evaluate operational decisions.

Commodity markets adjust expectations.

Financial institutions monitor potential economic implications.

The Strait therefore functions not merely as a transportation corridor.

It also serves as an economic barometer.

## Risk Premiums

Economists frequently distinguish between price and risk.

Two identical assets may command different market values if one carries greater uncertainty.

This difference is known as a risk premium.

Energy markets exhibit this principle regularly.

Periods of heightened uncertainty may contribute to higher transportation costs.

Insurance premiums.

Financing expenses.

Commodity prices.

These additional costs represent compensation for increased uncertainty rather than changes in the underlying physical commodity itself.

Risk therefore possesses measurable economic value.

Managing uncertainty becomes an important component of efficient markets.

## Investment and Long-Term Stability

Large energy projects require extraordinary amounts of capital.

Exploration.

Production facilities.

Refineries.

Pipelines.

Ports.

Shipping fleets.

Each requires billions of dollars in long-term investment.

Such projects often operate for decades.

Investors therefore evaluate political stability alongside expected financial returns.

Countries characterized by transparent institutions, reliable legal systems, sound regulatory environments, and predictable commercial policies generally attract greater long-term investment.

Institutional quality becomes an economic asset.

Confidence encourages capital formation.

Capital formation supports productivity.

Productivity generates prosperity.

## The Importance of International Cooperation

Many geopolitical risks cannot be addressed by individual nations acting alone.

International commerce depends upon cooperation.

Diplomatic dialogue.

Trade agreements.

Maritime coordination.

Information sharing.

Regional partnerships.

International institutions.

These mechanisms reduce uncertainty by encouraging communication, transparency, and peaceful dispute resolution.

From an economic perspective, successful cooperation lowers transaction costs.

It strengthens investor confidence.

It promotes long-term commercial relationships.

Ultimately, stable international relationships support more efficient global markets.

Economic Reflection

Risk has always accompanied commerce.

Ancient merchants feared storms.

Modern businesses evaluate financial markets, transportation networks, regulatory environments, and geopolitical developments.

Although the sources of uncertainty have evolved, the underlying economic principle remains remarkably constant.

Prosperity flourishes where confidence exceeds fear.

Investment expands where institutions remain reliable.

Trade grows where transportation remains secure.

The Strait of Hormuz demonstrates how geography, diplomacy, economics, and international commerce converge within a single strategic location.

Its importance reminds us that markets do not respond solely to production and consumption.

They also respond to expectations.

Confidence.

Institutional strength.

And the collective belief that commerce will continue moving peacefully across the world's oceans.

The most valuable commodity within any economy is not merely oil.

It is confidence.

Without confidence, investment hesitates.

Without investment, growth slows.

With confidence, however, nations build industries, businesses expand, innovation accelerates, and prosperity becomes sustainable.

Key Economic Takeaways

- Geopolitical risk refers to political and strategic developments that may influence economic activity.
- Markets generally reward stability and respond negatively to increased uncertainty.
- Energy markets are particularly sensitive to geopolitical developments because of their global interconnectedness.
- Risk premiums reflect the additional costs associated with uncertainty rather than changes in physical supply alone.
- Strong institutions, international cooperation, and secure commercial transportation contribute significantly to investor confidence, economic resilience, and long-term global prosperity.

“Markets rise when confidence rises, and confidence grows where stability endures. Geopolitical risk reminds us that prosperity is never automatic—it is earned through secure institutions, steady commerce, and the protection of vital routes that keep the world connected."

— Dr. Sofia Lindgren, Geopolitical Risk Economist

## CHAPTER XV
## Financial Markets and Energy Price Volatility

Financial markets are often described as the nervous system of the global economy.

Every second, investors analyze information from every corner of the world.

Economic reports.

Corporate earnings.

Interest rates.

Employment figures.

Trade balances.

Technological innovations.

Geopolitical developments.

Commodity prices.

Each new piece of information influences expectations regarding future economic performance.

Among all internationally traded commodities, few receive as much attention as crude oil.

Its price is followed not only by energy companies but also by airlines, manufacturers, banks, central banks, shipping firms, pension funds, governments, and individual investors.

Oil has become one of the world's most influential economic indicators.

Understanding its price movements therefore provides valuable insight into the broader behavior of global financial markets.

## Markets Look Forward

One of the defining characteristics of financial markets is that they are forward-looking.

Investors rarely make decisions based solely upon present conditions.

Instead, they attempt to anticipate future developments.

Will economic growth accelerate?

Will industrial production expand?

Will consumer demand increase?

Will inflation remain stable?

Will energy supplies remain sufficient?

These expectations influence today's investment decisions.

Consequently, financial markets often react long before measurable economic changes occur.

Expectations become incorporated into asset prices almost immediately.

## Oil as an Economic Signal

The price of crude oil communicates valuable information.

Rising prices may reflect stronger global demand.

They may indicate tightening supply.

They may incorporate higher transportation costs.

They may also reflect changing expectations regarding future market conditions.

Similarly, declining prices may result from expanding production, slowing economic activity, technological improvements, or changes in consumer demand.

Economists therefore analyze oil prices carefully.

They provide insight not only into energy markets but also into broader patterns of global economic activity.

Oil prices function as one of the world's most closely watched economic signals.

## Commodity Markets and Price Discovery

Modern commodity exchanges perform an essential economic function.

They facilitate what economists call price discovery.

Thousands of buyers and sellers continuously negotiate prices based upon available information.

No single participant determines market prices.

Instead, prices emerge through the interaction of millions of individual decisions.

Producers seek profitable returns.

Consumers seek affordable supplies.

Investors evaluate future expectations.

Financial institutions provide liquidity.

Together, these participants create markets capable of rapidly incorporating new information.

Price discovery contributes to efficient resource allocation throughout the economy.

Volatility Is Not the Same as Instability

Financial commentators frequently associate volatility with crisis.

Economists make an important distinction.

Volatility simply refers to changes in prices over time.

Markets naturally fluctuate as new information becomes available.

Moderate volatility reflects healthy market adjustment.

Persistent instability, however, occurs when uncertainty becomes sufficiently significant to impair investment, production, or commercial planning.

Well-functioning markets absorb information continuously.

Price movements help allocate resources toward their most productive uses.

Volatility therefore performs an important economic function when supported by transparent markets and reliable institutions.

## The Influence of Interest Rates

Energy markets and financial markets are closely connected through monetary policy.

When inflation accelerates, central banks may adjust interest rates to promote price stability.

Interest rates influence borrowing costs.

Investment decisions.

Consumer spending.

Business expansion.

Housing markets.

Currency values.

These changes can indirectly affect future energy demand.

Likewise, sustained changes in energy prices may influence inflation expectations, creating an important interaction between commodity markets and monetary policy.

This relationship illustrates the interconnected nature of macroeconomics.

No major market operates independently.

Investment in the Energy Sector

The petroleum industry requires substantial long-term investment.

Exploration.

Production facilities.

Offshore platforms.

Pipelines.

Refineries.

Shipping fleets.

Storage terminals.

Each project requires significant financial capital.

Investors evaluate expected returns over many years rather than weeks or months.

Stable financial markets encourage capital formation.

Predictable regulatory environments strengthen investment confidence.

Reliable transportation infrastructure supports long-term planning.

The continued operation of strategic maritime corridors, including the Strait of Hormuz, therefore contributes indirectly to investment throughout the global energy industry.

## Global Financial Integration

Financial markets today operate within an extraordinarily interconnected international system.

Banks finance international trade.

Institutional investors allocate capital across continents.

Pension funds invest globally.

Insurance companies diversify portfolios.

Multinational corporations raise financing through international capital markets.

Energy companies participate in this integrated financial ecosystem alongside manufacturers, technology firms, transportation companies, and governments.

Developments affecting one sector frequently influence many others.

This interconnectedness explains why energy markets receive such careful attention from economists, policymakers, and investors worldwide.

## The Strait of Hormuz and Market Confidence

The Strait of Hormuz represents more than a maritime passage.

Within financial markets, it symbolizes one of the principal transportation corridors supporting global energy commerce.

Its continued accessibility contributes to confidence regarding future energy supplies.

Confidence encourages investment.

Investment supports production.

Production promotes employment.

Employment strengthens economic growth.

Although financial markets evaluate countless variables simultaneously, reliable transportation infrastructure remains among the most important foundations supporting long-term economic confidence.

The Strait of Hormuz quietly fulfills that role every day.

Economic Reflection

Financial markets are often misunderstood as institutions driven solely by speculation.

In reality, they perform one of the most important functions within modern economies.

They allocate capital.

They evaluate risk.

They finance innovation.

They support entrepreneurship.

They facilitate long-term investment.

Energy markets illustrate these functions particularly well.

The price of oil reflects not only current production but also expectations regarding future prosperity.

Every investment in energy infrastructure represents confidence in continued economic development.

Every efficient shipping route supports market stability.

Every secure maritime corridor strengthens the international commercial system.

The Strait of Hormuz reminds us that financial markets ultimately depend upon the same principle that has guided commerce for centuries:

Confidence.

When confidence is supported by sound institutions, secure transportation, open markets, and responsible economic policy, capital flows, businesses expand, innovation flourishes, and prosperity grows.

The world's financial markets may appear to operate through numbers displayed on computer screens.

Yet beneath every transaction lies something far more fundamental.

The movement of commerce.

And the confidence that tomorrow's voyage will arrive safely.

Key Economic Takeaways

- Financial markets are forward-looking and incorporate expectations regarding future economic conditions.
- Oil prices serve as important indicators of global economic activity and market expectations.
- Commodity markets facilitate efficient price discovery through the interaction of buyers and sellers.
- Moderate price volatility is a natural characteristic of efficient markets and differs from prolonged economic instability.

- Stable energy transportation networks, including the Strait of Hormuz, contribute to investor confidence, long-term capital formation, and the efficient functioning of global financial markets.

"Energy prices move markets, but confidence moves civilizations. When transportation remains secure and information flows freely, volatility becomes manageable and financial systems continue to support global prosperity."
— Dr. Marcellus Grant, Financial Markets Economist

# CHAPTER XVI
## Technology, Pipelines, and Alternative Routes

Technology has always reshaped the global economy.

The steam engine transformed manufacturing.

Railroads connected continents.

Electricity revolutionized industry.

The internet accelerated the exchange of information.

Artificial intelligence is now redefining productivity across multiple sectors.

The energy industry has experienced similar waves of innovation.

Advances in exploration, drilling, transportation, engineering, and digital technology have dramatically increased efficiency while expanding access to previously inaccessible resources.

Yet one economic reality remains unchanged.

Technology may improve production.

It cannot alter geography.

Pipelines can reduce transportation distances.

Engineering can improve efficiency.

Ships can become larger and more sophisticated.

But strategic maritime chokepoints continue to occupy positions that no innovation has entirely replaced.

The Strait of Hormuz remains one of the clearest examples of this enduring relationship between technological progress and geographic permanence.

## The Technological Evolution of Energy

The petroleum industry of the twenty-first century differs remarkably from that of a century ago.

Modern seismic imaging enables geologists to identify underground formations with extraordinary precision.

Advanced drilling techniques have improved recovery rates while reducing operational costs.

Digital monitoring systems enhance safety, increase efficiency, and optimize production.

Artificial intelligence assists engineers in forecasting maintenance needs, improving logistics, and analyzing enormous quantities of operational data.

These innovations have strengthened productivity throughout the global energy industry.

Technology has become one of the principal drivers of economic efficiency.

## Pipelines: Expanding Transportation Options

Pipelines represent one of the most efficient methods of transporting oil and natural gas across land.

Unlike maritime transportation, pipelines operate continuously.

They reduce dependence upon trucks and rail transportation.

They lower handling costs.

They provide reliable delivery schedules.

For producing nations, pipelines offer valuable flexibility by connecting energy fields directly with refineries, export terminals, or domestic consumers.

From an economic perspective, pipelines diversify transportation infrastructure and improve system resilience.

Diversification reduces vulnerability.

Resilience strengthens long-term stability.

Alternative Export Routes

Recognizing the strategic importance of maritime chokepoints, several energy-producing countries have invested in alternative transportation corridors.

Some pipelines allow portions of oil production to reach ports located outside the Persian Gulf.

Others connect inland production with different coastal terminals.

These projects increase flexibility.

They reduce transportation bottlenecks.

They enhance emergency planning.

However, economics requires careful evaluation of trade-offs.

Pipeline construction demands enormous capital investment.

Engineering complexity.

Environmental planning.

Long-term maintenance.

Political cooperation.

Even when alternative routes exist, they often possess lower transportation capacity than major maritime shipping lanes.

As a result, alternative infrastructure generally complements rather than replaces established sea routes.

## Technology and Maritime Shipping

Innovation has also transformed commercial shipping.

Modern oil tankers are larger, safer, and more fuel-efficient than previous generations.

Advanced navigation systems improve voyage planning.

Satellite communications enhance operational awareness.

Digital logistics platforms optimize cargo scheduling.

Predictive maintenance reduces equipment failures.

Environmental technologies improve fuel efficiency while reducing emissions.

Each advancement contributes to lower transportation costs and greater operational reliability.

The cumulative effect is significant.

More efficient shipping strengthens international trade and supports long-term economic growth.

## Energy Diversification

Many countries are pursuing broader energy diversification strategies.

Renewable energy.

Hydroelectric generation.

Nuclear power.

Natural gas.

Hydrogen technologies.

Energy storage systems.

Each contributes to a more diversified energy portfolio.

Diversification does not eliminate petroleum from the global economy.

Rather, it broadens the range of available energy sources.

Economically, diversification reduces concentration risk.

A diversified energy system possesses greater flexibility when responding to changing market conditions, technological innovation, or evolving consumer preferences.

## The Limits of Technology

Technological progress has solved countless economic challenges.

It has expanded production.

Reduced costs.

Improved safety.

Increased efficiency.

Yet certain realities remain beyond technological control.

Geography remains constant.

The shortest maritime routes remain the shortest maritime routes.

Natural harbors remain strategically valuable.

Mountain ranges continue influencing pipeline construction.

Narrow waterways continue channeling international commerce.

Technology enhances the utilization of geography.

It does not eliminate geography itself.

This distinction remains fundamental to understanding the continuing importance of the Strait of Hormuz.

## Innovation and Economic Competitiveness

Technological leadership contributes significantly to national competitiveness.

Countries investing in research, engineering, infrastructure, education, and innovation often experience higher productivity growth over time.

The energy sector reflects this principle clearly.

Advances in exploration techniques improve production efficiency.

Digital technologies optimize logistics.

Automation enhances operational reliability.

Engineering innovation reduces transportation costs.

Productivity gains strengthen economic competitiveness throughout the broader economy.

Innovation therefore represents both an economic asset and a strategic advantage.

## The Future of Transportation Infrastructure

Looking ahead, transportation infrastructure will continue evolving.

Smarter ports.

Autonomous vessel technologies.

Artificial intelligence.

Digital supply chain management.

Improved environmental performance.

Greater operational efficiency.

These developments will reshape global commerce during the coming decades.

Nevertheless, the underlying structure of international trade will continue relying upon strategic transportation corridors connecting producers with consumers.

Technology will improve these networks.

It is unlikely to replace them entirely.

The Strait of Hormuz will therefore remain an indispensable component of global energy logistics for many years to come.

Economic Reflection

History demonstrates that technological innovation consistently expands economic opportunity.

It increases productivity.

Reduces costs.

Creates new industries.

Improves living standards.

Yet innovation succeeds most effectively when combined with favorable geography, reliable institutions, efficient infrastructure, and open markets.

Technology does not compete with geography.

It complements it.

Pipelines strengthen transportation flexibility.

Advanced ships improve maritime efficiency.

Artificial intelligence enhances operational performance.

Together, these innovations make the global energy system more productive and resilient.

The Strait of Hormuz remains at the center of this evolving system.

Not because technology has failed.

But because geography continues to define the pathways through which global commerce flows.

The lesson is timeless.

Innovation transforms economies.

Geography anchors them.

The greatest prosperity emerges when both work together.

Key Economic Takeaways

- Technological innovation has significantly improved energy production, transportation, and operational efficiency.
- Pipelines diversify transportation infrastructure and strengthen energy system resilience.
- Alternative export routes complement rather than fully replace major maritime corridors.
- Energy diversification reduces long-term economic risk while improving flexibility.
- Despite continuous technological progress, geography remains a permanent determinant of global trade, ensuring the continued strategic importance of the Strait of Hormuz.

"Technology can redirect the flow of energy, but geography decides the path. Prosperity follows when innovation strengthens the routes that nature has already chosen."
— Dr. Aurelia Han, Energy Systems Economist

## CHAPTER XVII
## The Future of Oil in an Energy Transition

The global economy is entering one of the most significant energy transitions since the Industrial Revolution.

Around the world, governments, businesses, universities, entrepreneurs, and investors are developing new technologies designed to diversify the world's energy portfolio.

Renewable energy.

Advanced nuclear reactors.

Hydrogen.

Carbon capture technologies.

Battery storage.

Artificial intelligence.

Smart electrical grids.

Each represents an important chapter in the evolution of global energy.

Yet every economic transition requires time.

History demonstrates that major changes in energy systems occur gradually rather than suddenly.

Coal did not disappear with the discovery of oil.

Nor did petroleum immediately replace every previous source of energy.

Instead, new technologies were integrated alongside existing ones as economies adapted to changing needs.

The transition currently underway follows a similar pattern.

Understanding this process requires economic analysis rather than ideological debate.

## The Economics of Energy Transitions

Energy transitions are among the most capital-intensive transformations an economy can undertake.

Power plants must be constructed.

Transmission systems expanded.

Research funded.

Manufacturing facilities modernized.

Transportation infrastructure upgraded.

Entire industries gradually adapt to emerging technologies.

These investments require decades rather than years.

Markets therefore evolve progressively.

Businesses balance innovation with reliability.

Consumers adopt new technologies according to affordability, convenience, and infrastructure availability.

Governments establish regulatory frameworks designed to facilitate orderly transitions.

Economic evolution occurs through investment rather than abrupt replacement.

## The Continuing Role of Petroleum

Despite remarkable advances in alternative energy technologies, petroleum continues to occupy an essential position within the global economy.

Commercial aviation depends heavily upon liquid fuels.

International shipping continues to rely substantially on petroleum products.

Heavy construction equipment, mining operations, petrochemical manufacturing, and numerous industrial processes remain closely connected to hydrocarbons.

In addition, petroleum serves as an important raw material for products extending far beyond transportation.

Medical equipment.

Pharmaceuticals.

Synthetic materials.

Industrial chemicals.

Packaging.

Consumer products.

Modern civilization continues to utilize petroleum in countless applications.

The future of energy therefore involves diversification rather than simple substitution.

Renewable Energy and Economic Opportunity

Renewable energy technologies have expanded significantly during the past several decades.

Solar generation.

Wind power.

Hydroelectric facilities.

Geothermal resources.

Battery storage.

Each contributes to expanding the diversity of global energy supplies.

From an economic perspective, innovation creates opportunity.

New industries emerge.

Employment expands.

Engineering advances.

Manufacturing capacity grows.

Investment accelerates.

Technological progress has historically strengthened productivity while creating entirely new sectors of economic activity.

The energy transition offers similar possibilities.

Innovation and economic growth often reinforce one another.

## The Importance of Energy Diversity

Economists generally recognize that diversified systems tend to be more resilient.

Investors diversify portfolios.

Businesses diversify suppliers.

Nations similarly benefit from diversified energy systems.

No single energy source perfectly satisfies every economic need.

Different industries possess different requirements.

Different countries possess different natural resources.

Different regions possess different geographic advantages.

Consequently, the future global energy system will likely consist of multiple complementary technologies working together.

Diversification enhances flexibility.

Flexibility strengthens resilience.

Resilience supports long-term prosperity.

## The Strait of Hormuz During the Energy Transition

Some observers assume that the expansion of renewable energy will eliminate the strategic importance of the Strait of Hormuz.

Economic analysis suggests a more nuanced conclusion.

Even as alternative energy sources expand, global demand for petroleum and natural gas is expected to remain significant for many years across numerous industries.

Emerging economies continue to industrialize.

Global transportation networks remain extensive.

Petrochemical industries continue supplying products essential to modern life.

Consequently, international energy trade will continue requiring efficient transportation infrastructure.

The Strait of Hormuz is therefore likely to remain one of the world's most important maritime corridors throughout much of the energy transition.

Its role may gradually evolve.

Its strategic importance is unlikely to disappear.

## Innovation as an Economic Constant

History demonstrates that innovation consistently reshapes markets.

Steam engines transformed manufacturing.

Electricity revolutionized industry.

Computers accelerated productivity.

Digital technologies connected global commerce.

Artificial intelligence is now creating another period of extraordinary transformation.

The energy sector will continue experiencing similar innovation.

The challenge for policymakers, businesses, and investors is not resisting change.

It is managing change responsibly.

Successful economies embrace innovation while preserving stability.

Balanced transitions encourage investment.

Predictable policies strengthen confidence.

Confidence supports sustainable economic development.

## The Human Dimension of Energy

Behind every technological breakthrough stand millions of people.

Scientists conducting research.

Engineers designing new systems.

Construction workers building infrastructure.

Entrepreneurs developing innovative companies.

Educators preparing future generations.

Investors providing capital.

Workers adapting to changing industries.

Economic transitions ultimately depend upon human creativity.

Technology is created by people.

Markets serve people.

Economic growth improves the lives of people.

This human dimension remains the most important aspect of every energy transition.

Economic Reflection

The history of economics is not the history of replacing one technology with another.

It is the history of expanding human opportunity through innovation.

Every generation inherits new tools.

New knowledge.

New industries.

New possibilities.

The energy transition currently underway represents another chapter in this remarkable story.

Petroleum helped build the modern industrial world.

Renewable technologies, advanced energy systems, and future innovations will help shape the decades ahead.

The objective should not be choosing one source of energy over another.

The objective is building an energy system that is reliable, affordable, resilient, innovative, and capable of supporting rising living standards for future generations.

The Strait of Hormuz will remain an important part of that journey.

Not because the future refuses to change...

But because economic progress builds upon existing foundations while creating new ones.

The world's energy future is not a destination.

It is an evolution.

And every successful evolution begins with sound economics.

Key Economic Takeaways

- Major energy transitions occur gradually and require substantial long-term investment.
- Petroleum is expected to remain an important component of the global economy alongside expanding alternative energy sources.
- Renewable energy creates new industries, employment opportunities, and technological innovation.
- Diversified energy systems improve resilience and strengthen long-term economic stability.
- The Strait of Hormuz is likely to remain strategically significant throughout the global energy transition because international commerce will continue relying on secure and efficient transportation corridors.

"Energy transitions reshape technology, but they do not erase the foundations of global commerce. Oil will remain part of the world's economic fabric as new systems rise beside it, not in place of it."
— Dr. Leandro Matsuoka, Energy Transition Economist

# CHAPTER XVIII
## Lessons for Policymakers and Business Leaders

Economic history is more than a record of prosperity and recession.

It is a laboratory of human decision-making.

Every financial crisis, technological revolution, energy transition, and geopolitical challenge offers valuable lessons for those entrusted with guiding economies and managing institutions.

Successful leaders understand that uncertainty cannot be eliminated.

It can only be anticipated, managed, and, when possible, transformed into opportunity.

The Strait of Hormuz offers one of the clearest case studies in applied economics because it demonstrates how geography, energy, commerce, finance, diplomacy, and national strategy converge within a single economic system.

Its lessons extend far beyond governments.

They are equally relevant to business executives, investors, entrepreneurs, economists, and future policymakers.

Lesson One: Geography Still Matters

Modern technology has connected continents with unprecedented speed.

Digital communication occurs instantaneously.

Financial transactions settle within seconds.

Artificial intelligence processes information at extraordinary scales.

Yet physical commerce continues to depend upon geography.

Ships still navigate oceans.

Pipelines still cross mountains.

Ports still connect nations.

Strategic waterways still influence international trade.

Economic policy that ignores geography risks misunderstanding the structural realities that shape global markets.

The map remains one of the economist's most valuable analytical tools.

Lesson Two: Markets Reward Stability

Businesses make investments based upon expectations.

Factories require years to construct.

Ports require decades to expand.

Energy infrastructure represents long-term capital commitments.

Investors therefore seek environments characterized by predictable institutions, transparent regulations, sound legal systems, and stable commercial relationships.

Stability encourages entrepreneurship.

Entrepreneurship increases productivity.

Productivity raises living standards.

Economic growth is built upon confidence.

Maintaining that confidence remains one of the foremost responsibilities of public institutions.

Lesson Three: Diversification Creates Resilience

No successful investment portfolio depends upon a single asset.

Likewise, resilient economies rarely depend upon a single industry, supplier, transportation route, or energy source.

Diversification reduces vulnerability.

Businesses diversify production.

Governments diversify energy supplies.

Financial institutions diversify investments.

Supply chains diversify logistics.

The objective is not to eliminate risk.

It is to prevent any single disruption from producing disproportionate economic consequences.

The principle of diversification remains one of the most enduring concepts in economics.

Lesson Four: Infrastructure Is an Investment

Infrastructure is often viewed merely as public expenditure.

Economically, it is productive capital.

Ports increase trade.

Highways improve logistics.

Railroads expand markets.

Airports facilitate commerce.

Pipelines strengthen energy distribution.

Digital infrastructure accelerates productivity.

Each investment increases the productive capacity of an economy.

Infrastructure should therefore be evaluated not only by its construction cost but also by the economic opportunities it creates over generations.

Lesson Five: International Trade Is a Partnership

No nation produces everything it consumes.

No economy possesses every natural resource.

International trade allows countries to specialize according to comparative advantage while benefiting from the strengths of others.

Energy-producing nations support industrial economies.

Manufacturing countries produce goods for global markets.

Agricultural exporters contribute to food security.

Financial centers allocate investment capital.

This interdependence encourages cooperation through commerce.

Trade is not merely the exchange of products.

It is the exchange of opportunity.

Lesson Six: Risk Must Be Managed, Not Ignored

Every investment carries uncertainty.

Every market experiences cycles.

Every economy faces unexpected events.

Successful leaders acknowledge these realities without becoming paralyzed by them.

Risk management requires preparation.

Strategic planning.

Emergency reserves.

Diversified supply chains.

Financial discipline.

Institutional flexibility.

These principles strengthen resilience before adversity occurs.

Preparation consistently proves less expensive than recovery.

## Lesson Seven: Innovation Drives Long-Term Prosperity

The world's wealthiest economies consistently invest in knowledge.

Education.

Scientific research.

Engineering.

Technology.

Entrepreneurship.

Innovation increases productivity.

Productivity supports higher wages.

Higher wages improve living standards.

Long-term prosperity depends not only upon natural resources but also upon human creativity.

The greatest economic resource has always been the human mind.

## The Responsibility of Leadership

Leadership within economics extends beyond balancing budgets or increasing production.

True leadership requires vision.

It requires recognizing that today's decisions influence future generations.

Responsible policymakers consider long-term sustainability alongside short-term performance.

Responsible business leaders invest in people as well as profits.

Responsible institutions strengthen public confidence through transparency, accountability, and sound governance.

Economic leadership is ultimately measured not by quarterly statistics alone.

It is measured by the opportunities created for future generations.

## The Strait of Hormuz as a Classroom

The Strait of Hormuz teaches lessons extending far beyond maritime commerce.

It demonstrates the value of secure transportation.

The importance of stable institutions.

The necessity of international cooperation.

The significance of infrastructure.

The relationship between geography and economics.

The importance of prudent risk management.

Few places on Earth illustrate so many economic principles simultaneously.

For students of economics, it is more than a strategic waterway.

It is a living classroom.

Economic Reflection

The world's economy has become increasingly interconnected.

A decision made in one nation may influence industries across multiple continents.

A technological innovation developed in one laboratory may transform global productivity.

A commercial vessel passing through the Strait of Hormuz may carry the energy that powers factories, hospitals, schools, businesses, and homes thousands of miles away.

These realities remind us that economics is ultimately the study of cooperation.

Markets function because millions of individuals voluntarily exchange goods, services, knowledge, and capital.

Institutions exist to support that cooperation.

Infrastructure enables it.

Innovation strengthens it.

Leadership preserves it.

The future prosperity of the global economy will depend not only upon abundant resources but also upon wise decisions.

The economist's responsibility is therefore greater than explaining markets.

It is helping society understand how sound institutions, responsible leadership, and peaceful commerce can create lasting prosperity.

That is perhaps the greatest lesson the Strait of Hormuz has to offer.

Key Economic Takeaways

- Geography continues to influence economic development despite rapid technological progress.

- Stable institutions encourage investment, entrepreneurship, and long-term economic growth.
- Diversification strengthens resilience across energy systems, supply chains, and financial markets.
- Infrastructure should be viewed as productive capital that generates future economic opportunity.
- Sound leadership, innovation, international trade, and prudent risk management remain essential pillars of sustainable prosperity in the twenty-first century.

"Prosperity is not an accident. It is the result of leaders who respect geography, invest in infrastructure, manage risk wisely, and build institutions strong enough to support the ambitions of future generations."
— Dr. Rafael Moretti, Strategic Economics Investigator

## CHAPTER XIX
## The Strait of Hormuz and the Twenty-First Century World Economy

The twenty-first century is defined by interdependence.

Never before have nations been so economically connected.

A semiconductor designed in one country may be manufactured in another, assembled in a third, transported across several oceans, and purchased by consumers on the opposite side of the world.

Raw materials extracted from one continent become finished products on another.

Capital flows across international financial markets within seconds.

Information moves almost instantaneously.

Yet despite these extraordinary technological achievements, one reality remains unchanged.

Physical commerce still depends upon physical geography.

Ships must still cross oceans.

Cargo must still pass through ports.

Energy must still reach consumers.

Among all the world's strategic maritime corridors, few illustrate this reality more powerfully than the Strait of Hormuz.

It remains one of the indispensable gateways connecting energy-producing nations with the global economy.

Its influence extends far beyond regional politics.

It affects international finance, industrial production, global trade, monetary policy, investment, and economic growth.

Understanding the modern world requires understanding the importance of this remarkable waterway.

## The Artery of Global Energy

Every day, enormous quantities of petroleum and liquefied natural gas transit the Strait of Hormuz before continuing toward major consumer markets around the world.

This uninterrupted movement of energy supports industries employing millions of people.

Airlines transport passengers across continents.

Factories manufacture automobiles, machinery, electronics, pharmaceuticals, and countless consumer products.

Power plants generate electricity.

Agricultural equipment cultivates food.

Commercial shipping connects international markets.

The energy moving through this narrow passage quietly sustains a significant portion of the world's productive capacity.

Few locations possess such widespread economic influence.

## Globalization and Economic Interdependence

Globalization has transformed isolated national economies into an interconnected international marketplace.

Trade has expanded dramatically.

Foreign investment has accelerated.

Technological innovation has spread rapidly across borders.

Consumers enjoy greater product availability than at any previous period in history.

This remarkable integration has generated extraordinary economic opportunities.

It has also increased the importance of resilient supply chains and reliable transportation infrastructure.

The Strait of Hormuz represents one of the principal links within this global commercial network.

Its continued accessibility supports the uninterrupted movement of one of the world's most essential commodities.

## Energy and Economic Competitiveness

Affordable and reliable energy strengthens national competitiveness.

Manufacturers benefit from predictable production costs.

Transportation companies operate more efficiently.

Agricultural productivity increases.

Industrial investment expands.

Consumers enjoy greater purchasing power.

Although many factors contribute to economic success, energy remains one of the most important productive inputs supporting modern economies.

Countries possessing reliable access to energy generally enjoy greater flexibility in supporting industrial development and long-term economic planning.

Consequently, the stability of international energy markets remains an important objective for governments, businesses, and investors alike.

## The Importance of Open Commerce

Economic history consistently demonstrates that nations prosper through commerce.

Trade encourages specialization.

Competition stimulates innovation.

Investment expands productive capacity.

Consumers benefit from greater choice and lower costs.

Open commercial relationships also encourage cooperation among nations by creating mutual economic interests.

The Strait of Hormuz supports this broader system by facilitating the lawful movement of internationally traded energy.

Its economic value therefore extends beyond the petroleum industry.

It strengthens the broader framework upon which international commerce depends.

## The Role of Institutions

Markets perform most effectively when supported by strong institutions.

Transparent legal systems.

Reliable financial markets.

Efficient regulatory frameworks.

Stable governments.

Independent courts.

Secure property rights.

Responsible fiscal and monetary policies.

Together, these institutions create an environment where businesses invest confidently and entrepreneurs innovate freely.

The same principle applies internationally.

Predictable rules governing maritime commerce strengthen confidence throughout the global trading system.

Institutional stability remains one of the greatest competitive advantages any economy can possess.

## Economic Cooperation and Shared Prosperity

The world's largest economic achievements have rarely resulted from isolation.

They have emerged through cooperation.

Commercial partnerships.

Scientific collaboration.

International investment.

Technological exchange.

Educational advancement.

Peaceful trade.

The Strait of Hormuz illustrates this principle every day.

Energy exported through its waters supports factories thousands of miles away.

Those factories produce goods shipped to consumers across every inhabited continent.

The resulting prosperity benefits producers, manufacturers, transportation companies, financial institutions, retailers, workers, and consumers alike.

Global commerce succeeds because millions of individuals cooperate through voluntary exchange.

## The Enduring Importance of Geography

Technological progress has transformed nearly every aspect of modern civilization.

Artificial intelligence accelerates decision-making.

Digital finance connects global capital markets.

Automation increases industrial productivity.

Advanced engineering improves transportation efficiency.

Yet geography continues to shape economic opportunity.

Natural harbors remain valuable.

Major ports remain indispensable.

Strategic waterways continue influencing world trade.

The Strait of Hormuz demonstrates that geography remains one of the few constants within an ever-changing global economy.

Innovation changes how commerce operates.

Geography continues determining where commerce flows.

Economic Reflection

The Strait of Hormuz is more than a passage connecting two bodies of water.

It is a symbol of globalization itself.

It reminds us that modern prosperity depends upon cooperation across nations, industries, and institutions.

It demonstrates that economic growth requires not only production but also transportation.

Not only investment but also confidence.

Not only technology but also geography.

Its waters quietly sustain one of the world's most important commercial systems.

Every successful voyage reinforces international trade.

Every safely delivered shipment strengthens global supply chains.

Every uninterrupted flow of energy supports economic opportunity for millions of families around the world.

The economist who studies the Strait of Hormuz discovers far more than maritime geography.

He discovers the remarkable interconnectedness of modern civilization.

And perhaps the greatest lesson of all.

The prosperity of the twenty-first century will belong not merely to those who possess resources.

It will belong to those who protect commerce, encourage innovation, strengthen institutions, and recognize that peaceful economic cooperation remains one of humanity's greatest achievements.

Key Economic Takeaways

- The twenty-first-century economy is characterized by unprecedented global interdependence.
- Reliable energy transportation remains essential for industrial production, international trade, and economic growth.
- Open commerce, supported by strong institutions, encourages innovation, investment, and long-term prosperity.
- Geography continues to influence global trade despite rapid technological advancement.

- The Strait of Hormuz remains one of the world's most strategically significant economic corridors, connecting energy markets with the broader international economy and reinforcing the foundations of global prosperity.

"Global prosperity rests on the quiet reliability of the world's great trade routes. When energy moves freely and institutions remain strong, the entire international economy gains the confidence it needs to grow."
— Dr. Elias Navarro, World Economy Investigator

# CHAPTER XX
## The Future of Global Prosperity

Every generation inherits a world shaped by those who came before it.

The roads we travel.

The ports that receive commerce.

The pipelines that transport energy.

The institutions that protect markets.

The ships that cross the oceans.

The financial systems that allocate capital.

None appeared by accident.

They are the product of vision.

Investment.

Innovation.

Sacrifice.

And above all...

The enduring belief that cooperation creates greater prosperity than isolation.

The Strait of Hormuz stands as one of the greatest reminders of that truth.

For centuries, geography quietly waited.

Then humanity discovered the extraordinary wealth lying beneath the Persian Gulf.

Engineers unlocked it.

Entrepreneurs commercialized it.

Governments regulated it.

Investors financed it.

Workers produced it.

Mariners transported it.

Consumers utilized it.

Economists studied it.

Together, they transformed one narrow maritime passage into one of the principal arteries of the modern global economy.

No other waterway better illustrates the remarkable relationship between geography and economics.

The Greatest Economic Lesson

This book has examined oil.

Energy.

Transportation.

Shipping.

Insurance.

Financial markets.

Inflation.

Infrastructure.

Technology.

International trade.

National strategy.

Yet beneath every chapter lies one enduring principle.

Prosperity depends upon movement.

Goods must move.

Capital must move.

Ideas must move.

Innovation must move.

People must move.

Commerce must move.

When movement is interrupted...

Growth slows.

Investment hesitates.

Confidence weakens.

Opportunity diminishes.

The Strait of Hormuz reminds us that civilization advances when commerce flows freely.

## The Economics of Peace

History often remembers wars.

Economics remembers trade.

Wars consume wealth.

Commerce creates wealth.

Conflict destroys infrastructure.

Investment builds it.

Fear discourages entrepreneurship.

Confidence inspires innovation.

The greatest achievements of civilization have not been created upon battlefields.

They have been created in workshops.

Universities.

Factories.

Ports.

Research laboratories.

Financial institutions.

And marketplaces where free men and women voluntarily exchange goods, services, ideas, and knowledge.

Peace is not merely a humanitarian aspiration.

It is an extraordinary economic asset.

Stable societies attract investment.

Investment generates employment.

Employment creates prosperity.

Prosperity improves human dignity.

## The Responsibility of Great Nations

Throughout history, prosperous nations have carried responsibilities extending beyond their own borders.

Strong economies contribute to global financial stability.

Technological innovation benefits humanity.

Secure trade routes facilitate international commerce.

Reliable institutions strengthen confidence.

The United States has long been one of the world's leading economic powers.

Its entrepreneurs have transformed industries.

Its universities have advanced scientific discovery.

Its financial markets have allocated capital throughout the global economy.

Its institutions have influenced international commerce for generations.

Working alongside allies, trading partners, and international institutions, the United States has also participated in broader efforts supporting the stability of maritime commerce upon which much of the world's economy depends.

History will continue evaluating these contributions.

Economists, however, recognize a broader principle.

When international commerce remains secure...

The benefits extend to nations across every continent.

## The Next Energy Revolution

The future will not resemble the past.

New technologies will emerge.

Artificial intelligence will reshape industries.

Renewable energy will continue expanding.

Nuclear innovation will advance.

Hydrogen technologies will mature.

Transportation will evolve.

Supply chains will become increasingly intelligent.

Markets will become more efficient.

Yet one reality will remain unchanged.

Civilizations will continue requiring reliable energy.

Commerce will continue requiring secure transportation.

Investment will continue requiring confidence.

The forms may evolve.

The principles will endure.

The Strait That Changed the World

Maps often deceive.

They emphasize size.

Economics emphasizes influence.

The Strait of Hormuz occupies only a small space upon the globe.

Yet its influence reaches every continent.

Every refinery.

Every shipping company.

Every airline.

Every manufacturer.

Every financial institution.

Every household purchasing fuel.

Its importance cannot be measured in miles.

It must be measured in opportunity.

In productivity.

In commerce.

In prosperity.

It demonstrates that the greatest economic forces often originate in the smallest places.

A Message to Future Economists

To every student who opens this book...

Never study economics as though it were merely mathematics.

Economics is the story of humanity.

It is the study of how people cooperate.

How societies create prosperity.

How institutions build confidence.

How innovation expands opportunity.

How freedom encourages enterprise.

And how geography quietly influences every decision civilization makes.

Never forget that behind every statistic stands a worker.

Behind every graph stands a family.

Behind every investment stands hope.

Behind every successful economy stands millions of individuals striving to build better lives.

Economics is ultimately about people.

Always has been.

Always will be.

## The Final Reflection

When historians write about the twenty-first century, they will undoubtedly describe astonishing technological progress.

Artificial intelligence.

Quantum computing.

Biotechnology.

Space exploration.

Advanced robotics.

Clean energy.

Digital finance.

These innovations will redefine the future.

Yet historians may also discover that one ancient truth never changed.

Commerce remained the foundation of civilization.

And commerce depended upon trust.

Trust in institutions.

Trust in contracts.

Trust in markets.

Trust in peaceful cooperation.

Trust that ships would continue sailing.

Trust that energy would continue flowing.

Trust that tomorrow would offer greater opportunity than today.

The Strait of Hormuz symbolizes that trust.

It reminds humanity that prosperity is not guaranteed.

It is built.

Protected.

Improved.

And passed from one generation to the next.

Final Economic Reflection

Throughout this journey we have discovered something far greater than the economics of one strategic waterway.

We have discovered the extraordinary relationship between geography, commerce, innovation, leadership, and human progress.

The Strait of Hormuz is not simply a passage connecting the Persian Gulf with the Indian Ocean.

It is a bridge connecting continents.

Industries.

Cultures.

Markets.

Nations.

And ultimately...

People.

Its waters carry more than oil.

They carry possibility.

They carry opportunity.

They carry the hopes of workers, entrepreneurs, engineers, sailors, investors, manufacturers, scientists, and families whose lives are connected through peaceful commerce.

That is the true economics of Hormuz.

Not merely barrels of oil.

Not merely shipping lanes.

Not merely financial markets.

But the remarkable ability of free people, working across nations and generations, to create prosperity through cooperation rather than conflict.

If this book leaves the reader with one enduring lesson, let it be this:

The wealth of nations is not measured solely by the resources beneath their soil.

It is measured by the wisdom with which they use those resources, the strength of the institutions that protect commerce, the innovation that expands opportunity, and the determination of their people to build a more prosperous future.

For geography may shape destiny...

But it is human ingenuity, economic freedom, responsible leadership, and peaceful cooperation that transform destiny into civilization.

And so, as we close this study of one of the world's most important waterways, we are reminded that the future of global prosperity will never be determined by a single nation, a single resource, or a single generation.

It will be written by those who understand that the greatest force in history is neither war nor wealth...

It is the enduring power of commerce to unite humanity.

Finis.

"Prosperity endures when nations protect commerce, invest in innovation, and trust in the power of peaceful exchange. The future belongs to those who understand that cooperation is the greatest engine of human progress."
— Dr. Adrian Solari, Global Prosperity Economist

**Milton Rothbard's Final Note**

Every book an author writes reveals something about the subject.

This one also reveals something about the author.

I was not born into privilege.

I come from humble beginnings, where hard work was never optional—it was a necessity. I entered the workforce at a very young age to help support my family, a responsibility that taught me lessons no classroom could ever provide. Those early experiences shaped my understanding of work, personal responsibility, sacrifice, and the dignity that comes from earning one's way.

Decades later, that responsibility has never ended.

Today, I continue to work while serving as the caretaker of my elderly parents. My father, now ninety-seven years old, lives with Alzheimer's disease. My mother is ninety-one years old. Caring for them has been one of the greatest honors and responsibilities of my life. They cared for me when I was unable to care for myself. Today, I have the privilege of returning that love with gratitude.

If there is one lesson economics should never forget, it is that behind every statistic stands a human being.

Behind every labor market is a worker.

Behind every household is a family.

Behind every economy is the quiet determination of ordinary people striving to build better lives.

My intellectual journey has been equally demanding.

Knowledge is rarely acquired by accident.

It is earned through discipline, persistence, and countless hours of study.

For many years I sacrificed sleep, postponed meals, declined leisure, and surrendered precious family time in pursuit of a deeper understanding of economics, history, geopolitics, finance, and international trade. Those sacrifices were never made in pursuit of titles or recognition. They were made because I believe ideas matter, and because sound ideas have the power to improve lives.

My approach to economics has been profoundly influenced by some of the greatest thinkers of the modern era.

I have long admired Ludwig von Mises for his uncompromising defense of economic calculation and individual liberty.

Milton Friedman demonstrated the extraordinary power of free markets and the importance of monetary stability.

Murray Rothbard challenged readers to think deeply about liberty, property rights, and the proper role of government.

Thomas Sowell reminded us that economics is ultimately about incentives and the practical consequences of public policy.

Friedrich Hayek taught generations that knowledge is dispersed throughout society and that free individuals, acting voluntarily, often solve problems more effectively than centralized planning.

Their writings encouraged me to ask difficult questions, challenge accepted assumptions, and approach economics with intellectual curiosity and humility.

Readers will also discover that my own economic philosophy differs from both Keynesian economics and Marxism. Those are sincerely held convictions that have developed through years of study, professional experience, and reflection. I recognize that thoughtful economists reach different conclusions, and I encourage every reader to examine competing ideas carefully, consult original sources, and arrive at their own informed judgments.

This book was never intended merely to explain the economics of the Strait of Hormuz.

It was written to demonstrate how geography, energy, commerce, institutions, and human decision-making intersect to shape the prosperity of nations.

Economics is not simply about money.

It is about opportunity.

It is about productivity.

It is about innovation.

It is about responsibility.

Most importantly, it is about improving the human condition.

If these pages inspire even one student to study economics more deeply...

If they encourage one entrepreneur to pursue innovation...

If they help one policymaker appreciate the value of sound institutions...

Or if they remind one reader that knowledge is worth every sacrifice required to obtain it...

Then every late night, every missed meal, every hour of study, and every personal sacrifice will have been worthwhile.

I remain grateful to my family, whose love and patience have sustained me throughout this journey.

I remain grateful to my parents, whose example taught me perseverance, humility, and duty.

And I remain grateful to you, the reader.

Thank you for investing your most valuable resource—your time.

May you never stop asking questions.

May you never stop learning.

And may you always remember that the greatest investment any person can make is not in markets, currencies, or commodities...

It is in the relentless pursuit of knowledge, wisdom, and truth.

With sincere gratitude,

**Milton Rothbard**

## REFERENCES, INFLUENCES, AND ILLUSTRATIVE SOURCES

***A Curated Reference List for Further Study and Verification***

The following bibliography reflects the principal works, authors, institutions, and illustrative sources that informed, inspired, or are thematically related to the ideas presented throughout this book. Consistent with the Disclaimer, this work combines factual economic and geopolitical analysis with limited fictionalized and illustrative material designed to simplify complex concepts, protect confidential identities where appropriate, and enhance readability. Certain illustrative sources listed herein are intentionally identified as fictional or composite references.

This bibliography is intended to encourage readers to pursue further independent study in economics, energy markets, maritime commerce, geopolitics, international relations, and the enduring relationship between geography and global prosperity.

---

### Primary Authorial Works

Rothbard, Milton. *The Geography of Power.* Milton Rothbard Publishing.

Rothbard, Milton. *The Energy Reckoning.* Milton Rothbard Publishing.

Rothbard, Milton. *The Lithium Triangle.* Milton Rothbard Publishing.

Rothbard, Milton. *The Lithium Pact.* Milton Rothbard Publishing.

Rothbard, Milton. *The Hidden Architecture of Power.* Milton Rothbard Publishing.

---

### Economic Thinkers Who Influenced This Work

Friedman, Milton. *Capitalism and Freedom.* University of Chicago Press, 1962.

Hayek, Friedrich A. *The Road to Serfdom.* University of Chicago Press, 1944.

Mises, Ludwig von. *Human Action: A Treatise on Economics.* Yale University Press, 1949.
Rothbard, Murray N. *Man, Economy, and State.* D. Van Nostrand Company, 1962.
Sowell, Thomas. *Basic Economics.* Basic Books, 2000.
These distinguished economists profoundly influenced the analytical framework employed throughout this manuscript. While the conclusions presented are solely those of the author, the enduring contributions of these scholars to economic thought have provided invaluable intellectual guidance.

---

**Energy, Economics, and Global Markets**

Adelman, M. A. *The Economics of Petroleum Supply.* MIT Press, 1993.
International Energy Agency (IEA). *World Energy Outlook.* OECD Publishing.
BP. *Statistical Review of World Energy.* Annual Editions.
U.S. Energy Information Administration (EIA). *International Energy Outlook.* U.S. Department of Energy.
World Bank. *Global Economic Prospects.* World Bank Publications.

---

**Maritime Trade and International Shipping**

Stopford, Martin. *Maritime Economics.* Routledge.
Till, Geoffrey. *Seapower: A Guide for the Twenty-First Century.* Routledge.
United Nations Conference on Trade and Development (UNCTAD). *Review of Maritime Transport.* Annual Editions.
International Maritime Organization (IMO). *International Shipping Facts and Figures.* United Nations.

---

**Geography, Strategy, and International Affairs**

Kaplan, Robert D. *The Revenge of Geography.* Random House, 2012.
Mahan, Alfred Thayer. *The Influence of Sea Power upon History, 1660–1783.* Little, Brown and Company, 1890.
Kissinger, Henry. *World Order.* Penguin Press, 2014.
Allison, Graham. *Destined for War: Can America and China Escape Thucydides's Trap?* Houghton Mifflin Harcourt, 2017.
Nye, Joseph S. *The Future of Power.* PublicAffairs, 2011.

---

**Historical Foundations**

Gibbon, Edward. *The History of the Decline and Fall of the Roman Empire.* Strahan & Cadell, 1776–1789.

Additional historical information was derived from publicly available academic publications, governmental reports, historical archives, and internationally recognized reference materials.

---

**Illustrative and Fictional Composite Sources**

The following entries are intentionally fictionalized or composite references used solely for narrative illustration, educational examples, or the protection of identities, as disclosed in the Disclaimer.

Hale, Jonathan. *Strategic Maritime Notes.* Fictional composite reference.
Keating, Samuel. *Energy Corridors and Global Stability.* Fictional composite reference.
Ellery, Marcus. *Petroleum and Global Power.* Fictional composite reference.
Voskamp, Helena. *Inflation Dynamics and Maritime Trade.* Fictional composite reference.
Morimoto, Kenji. *Asia's Energy Future.* Fictional composite reference.
Navarro, Elias. *World Economy and Maritime Arteries.* Fictional composite reference.

Solari, Adrian. *Global Prosperity and Cooperation.* Fictional composite reference.
These references do not represent actual published works and are included solely for illustrative purposes consistent with the disclosures contained within this book.

---

**Primary Manuscript**

Rothbard, Milton.
*The Economics of Hormuz: Energy, Trade, Geopolitics, and the Waterway That Moves the World.*
Milton Rothbard Publishing, 2026.

---

**Author's Note on Sources**

Economics is a discipline built upon inquiry, evidence, debate, and the continuous pursuit of knowledge.

Readers are encouraged to consult the original works of the economists, historians, strategists, and institutions cited throughout this bibliography. No single book can encompass every perspective or every school of economic thought. Intellectual progress depends upon reading broadly, evaluating evidence critically, and engaging respectfully with differing viewpoints.

It is my sincere hope that this book serves not only as an introduction to the economics of the Strait of Hormuz, but also as an invitation to further explore the fascinating relationships among geography, energy, commerce, geopolitics, and the forces that shape the global economy.

— **Milton Rothbard**

www.ingramcontent.com/pod-product-compliance
Lightning Source LLC
LaVergne TN
LVHW022209200926
848481LV00006B/1909

* 9 7 9 8 9 5 1 1 5 3 7 0 8 *